Strategic Analysis of Air National Guard Combat Support and Reachback Functions

Robert S. Tripp, Kristin F. Lynch, Ronald G. McGarvey,

Don Snyder, Raymond A. Pyles, William A. Williams,

Charles Robert Roll, Jr.

Prepared for the United States Air Force

Approved for public release; distribution unlimited

PROJECT AIR FORCE

The research described in this report was sponsored by the United States Air Force under Contract F49642-01-C-0003. Further information may be obtained from the Strategic Planning Division, Directorate of Plans, Hq USAF.

Library of Congress Cataloging-in-Publication Data

Strategic analysis of Air National Guard combat support and reachback functions / Robert S. Tripp ... [et al.].
    p. cm.
    "MG-375."
    Includes bibliographical references.
    ISBN 0-8330-3884-2 (pbk. : alk. paper)
    1. United States—Air National Guard. 2. United States. Air Force—Equipment—Maintenance and repair. 3. Airplanes, Military—United States—Maintenance and repair. 4. United States. Air Force—Supplies and stores. 5. Opertational art (Military science) I. Tripp, Robert S., 1944–

UG1203.S77 2006
358.4'141—dc22

2006018940

Published 2006 by the RAND Corporation
1776 Main Street, P.O. Box 2138, Santa Monica, CA 90407-2138
1200 South Hayes Street, Arlington, VA 22202-5050
4570 Fifth Avenue, Suite 600, Pittsburgh, PA 15213
RAND URL: http://www.rand.org/
To order RAND documents or to obtain additional information, contact Distribution Services: Telephone: (310) 451-7002;
Fax: (310) 451-6915; Email: order@rand.org

Preface

The Air and Space Expeditionary Force (AEF), a concept developed by the Air Force, allows a quick response, when appropriate, to national security interests with a tailored, sustainable force. In this monograph, we focus on the needs of the Air Force, as a whole, for achieving the operational effects that enable the AEF, such as the ability to configure support rapidly and the ability to deploy and employ quickly. We concentrate on transformational opportunities for better meeting the needs of combat support missions for the AEF and on the role that the ANG may play in these transformational opportunities that would capitalize on ANG strengths and provide effective and efficient approaches to achieving the desired operational effects.

This monograph presents the results of our analysis of Air National Guard (ANG) combat support and reachback functions as part of four Air Force mission areas we evaluate:

- Civil engineering deployment and sustainment capabilities
- Continental United States (CONUS) Centralized Intermediate Repair Facilities
- GUARDIAN[1] capabilities
- Air and Space Operations Center reachback missions.

---

[1] GUARDIAN is an Air National Guard information system used to track and control execution of plans and operations, such as funding and performance data.

VANGUARD,[2] the new vision for the ANG, released in December 2002, calls for the ANG to evaluate new concepts, prepare for new missions, and adopt a new culture that leverages ANG strengths in meeting Air Force needs. The objective of the analysis was to ensure the ANG continues to play an important role in meeting the AEF mission. After evaluating each of the four Air Force mission areas, we evaluate where the ANG could effectively and efficiently aid in achieving AEF operational effects.

The Air National Guard Director of Logistics (ANG/LG) sponsored this research, which was conducted in the Resource Management Program of RAND Project AIR FORCE. The research for this monograph was completed in September 2004.

This report should be of interest to logisticians, operators, and mobility planners throughout the Department of Defense (DoD), especially those in the Air National Guard and active duty Air Force.

This report is one of a series of RAND reports that address agile combat support[3] (ACS) issues in implementing the AEF. Other publications issued as part of the larger project include the following:

- *Supporting Expeditionary Aerospace Forces: An Integrated Strategic Agile Combat Support Planning Framework,* Robert S. Tripp, Lionel A. Galway, Paul S. Killingsworth, Eric Peltz, Timothy L. Ramey, and John G. Drew (MR-1056-AF). This report describes an integrated combat support planning framework that may be used to evaluate support options on a continuing basis, particularly as technology, force structure, and threats change.
- *Supporting Expeditionary Aerospace Forces: New Agile Combat Support Postures,* Lionel Galway, Robert S. Tripp, Timothy L. Ramey, and John G. Drew (MR-1075-AF). This report describes how alternative resourcing of forward operating locations (FOLs) can support employment timelines for future AEF

---

[2] VANGUARD is the ANG long-range transformation program.

[3] An agile combat support system comprises forward support locations, CONUS support locations, forward operating locations, and robust command and control capabilities.

operations. It finds that rapid employment for combat requires some prepositioning of resources at FOLs.

- *Supporting Expeditionary Aerospace Forces: An Analysis of F-15 Avionics Options,* Eric Peltz, H. L. Shulman, Robert S. Tripp, Timothy L. Ramey, Randy King, and John G. Drew (MR-1174-AF). This report examines alternatives for meeting F-15 avionics maintenance requirements across a range of likely scenarios. The authors evaluate investments for new F-15 avionics intermediate shop-test equipment against several support options, including deploying maintenance capabilities with units, performing maintenance at forward support locations (FSLs), or performing all maintenance at the home station for deploying units.

- *Supporting Expeditionary Aerospace Forces: A Concept for Evolving to the Agile Combat Support/Mobility System of the Future,* Robert S. Tripp, Lionel A. Galway, Timothy L. Ramey, Mahyar A. Amouzegar, and Eric Peltz (MR-1179-AF). This report describes the vision for the ACS system of the future based on individual commodity study results.

- *Supporting Expeditionary Aerospace Forces: Expanded Analysis of LANTIRN Options,* Amatzia Feinberg, H. L. Shulman, L. W. Miller, and Robert S. Tripp (MR-1225-AF). This report examines alternatives for meeting low-altitude navigation and targeting infrared for night (LANTIRN) support requirements for AEF operations. The authors evaluate investments for new LANTIRN test equipment against several support options, including deploying maintenance capabilities with units, performing maintenance at FSLs, or performing all maintenance at continental United States (CONUS) support hubs for deploying units.

- *Supporting Expeditionary Aerospace Forces: Alternatives for Jet Engine Intermediate Maintenance,* Mahyar A. Amouzegar, Lionel A. Galway, and Amanda Geller (MR-1431-AF). This report evaluates the manner in which Jet Engine Intermediate Maintenance (JEIM) shops can best be configured to facilitate overseas deployments. The authors examine a number of JEIM support options, which are distinguished primarily by the degree to which JEIM support is centralized or decentralized. See also *Supporting Expeditionary Aerospace Forces: Engine Maintenance Systems Evaluation (En Masse): A Users Guide,* Mahyar A. Amouzegar and Lionel A. Galway (MR-1614-AF).

- *Supporting Expeditionary Aerospace Forces: An Operational Architecture for Combat Support Execution Planning and Control,* James A. Leftwich, Robert S. Tripp, Amanda Geller, Patrick H. Mills, Tom LaTourrette, C. Robert Roll, Jr., Cauley Von Hoffman, and David Johansen (MR-1536-AF). This report outlines the framework for evaluating options for combat support execution planning and control. The analysis describes the combat support command and control operational architecture as it is now and as it should be in the future. It also describes the changes that must take place to achieve that future state.

- *Reconfiguring Footprint to Speed Expeditionary Aerospace Forces Deployment,* Lionel A. Galway, Mahyar A. Amouzegar, R. J. Hillestad, and Don Snyder (MR-1625-AF). This study develops an analysis framework—footprint configuration—to assist in evaluating the feasibility of reducing the size of equipment or time-phasing the deployment of support and relocating some equipment to places other than forward operating locations. It also attempts to define *footprint* and to establish a way to monitor its reduction.

- *Analysis of Maintenance Forward Support Location Operations,* Amanda Geller, David Geroge, Robert S. Tripp, Mahyar A. Amouzegar, and C. Robert Roll, Jr. (MG-151-AF). This report discusses the conceptual development and recent implementation of maintenance forward support locations (also known as Centralized Intermediate Repair Facilities [CIRFs]) for the United States Air Force. The analysis focuses on the years leading up to and including the Deputy Chief of Staff for Installations and Logistics, U.S. Air Force (AF/IL) test of operations of CIRFs in the European theater from September 2001 to February 2002.

- *Supporting Air and Space Expeditionary Forces: Lessons from Operation Enduring Freedom,* Robert S. Tripp, Kristin F. Lynch, John G. Drew, and Edward W. Chan (MR-1819-AF). This report describes the expeditionary ACS experiences during the war in Afghanistan and compares these experiences with those associated with Joint Task Force Noble Anvil (JTF NA), the air war over Serbia. This report analyzes how ACS concepts were implemented, compares current experiences to determine similarities and unique practices, and indicates how well the ACS framework performed during these contingency operations. From this analysis, the ACS framework may be updated to better support the AEF concept.

- *Supporting Air and Space Expeditionary Forces: A Methodology for Determining Air Force Deployment Requirements,* Don Snyder and Patrick Mills (MG-176-AF). This report outlines a methodology for determining manpower and equipment deployment requirements. It describes a prototype policy analysis support tool based on this methodology, the Strategic Tool for the Analysis of Required Transportation (START); generates a list of capability units, called unit type codes (UTCs), that are required to support a user-specified operation; and determines movement characteristics. A fully implemented tool based on this prototype should prove to be useful to the Air Force in both deliberate and crisis action planning.

- *Supporting Air and Space Expeditionary Forces: Lessons from Operation Iraqi Freedom,* Kristin F. Lynch, John G. Drew, Robert S. Tripp, and C. Robert Roll, Jr. (MG-193-AF). This report describes the expeditionary ACS experiences during the war in Iraq and compares these experiences with those associated with Joint Task Force Noble Anvil (JTF NA), in Serbia, and Operation Enduring Freedom, in Afghanistan. It analyzes how combat support performed and how ACS concepts were implemented in Iraq, compares current experiences to determine similarities and unique practices, and indicates how well the ACS framework performed during these contingency operations.

- *Supporting Air and Space Expeditionary Forces: Analysis of Combat Support Basing Options,* Mahyar A. Amouzegar, Robert S. Tripp, Ronald G. McGarvey, Edward Wei-Min Chan, and Charles Robert Roll (MG-261-AF). This report evaluates a set of global FSL basing and transportation options for storing war reserve materiel. The authors present an analytical framework that can be used to evaluate alternative FSL options. A central component of the authors' framework is an optimization model that allows a user to select the best mix of land-based and sea-based FSLs for a given set of operational scenarios, thereby reducing costs while supporting a range of contingency operations.

RAND Project AIR FORCE

RAND Project AIR FORCE (PAF), a division of the RAND Corporation, is the U.S. Air Force's federally funded research and development center for studies and analyses. PAF provides the Air Force with independent analyses of policy alternatives affecting the development, employment, combat readiness, and support of current and future aerospace forces. Research is conducted in four programs: Aerospace Force Development; Manpower, Personnel, and Training; Resource Management; and Strategy and Doctrine.

Additional information about PAF is available on our Web site at http://www.rand.org/paf.

Contents

Figures

Tables

Summary

VANGUARD, the Air National Guard's (ANG's) long-range transformation program (released in December 2002), calls for the ANG to evaluate new concepts, prepare for new missions, and adopt a new culture that capitalizes on ANG strengths and ensures that the ANG continues to add value as warfighters and to warfighters in the future. One way to support warfighting and warfighters is to continue to support the Air and Space Expeditionary Force (AEF), a concept developed by the Air Force to allow quick response, when appropriate, to national security interests with a tailored, sustainable force. The ANG already plays an important role in the AEF during wartime operations. Here, we look at expanding that role both in peacetime and during operations.

In this monograph, we focus on operational effects, such as the ability to configure support rapidly and the ability to deploy and employ quickly, enabling the evolving AEF mission. Specifically, this analysis concentrates on options for combat support and reachback missions in four Air Force mission areas:

- Civil engineering deployment and sustainment capabilities
- Continental United States (CONUS) Centralized Intermediate Repair Facilities (CIRFs)

- The Force Structure and Cost Estimating Tool—A Planning Extension to GUARDIAN[1] capabilities
- Air and Space Operations Center (AOC) reachback missions.

More specifically, this project evaluates how fundamentally different policies, at the unit level and above the unit level, are likely to affect Total Force capabilities in meeting the needs of the AEF mission.

Through VANGUARD, the ANG has recognized the need to undertake a fundamental reexamination of its structure to ensure that it continues to play a leading role in meeting the AEF mission. After evaluating each of the four Air Force mission areas, we investigate transformational opportunities for the ANG that would add the most value in achieving the desired operational effects.

Civil Engineering Deployment and Sustainment Capabilities

The first chapter examines new deployment concepts using modified civil engineer (CE) unit type codes (UTCs). Using the current planning and deployment concept of Force Modules,[2] we modify CE UTCs to deploy and employ quickly in support of the AEF mission. In this transformational concept, a set of UTCs is deployed to perform the Establish the Base function, then is withdrawn. By modifying some CE UTCs in the Establish the Base Force Module, short but intense CE tasks are completed in one UTC, then personnel are withdrawn. A second UTC, composed of fewer personnel, would be created to provide continued CE Sustainment support. These concepts would open more opportunities for the ANG to accept CE tasks on a volunteer basis, and creating the Sustainment CE UTC would reduce active component requirements for sustaining tasks.

---

[1] GUARDIAN is an Air National Guard information system used to track and control execution of plans and operations, such as funding and performance data.

[2] Force Modules are sets of UTCs that define capabilities for creating and operating out of a deployed location.

We found that modifying some ANG UTCs, changing the deployment concept, and creating a separate Sustainment UTC might better support the AEF mission. The modified UTCs would provide intense CE support during a shorter deployment to establish the base. Then, a separate UTC would provide sustainment. These concepts could reduce active component deployment requirements as well as deployment and sustainment costs. (See pp. 9–32.)

CONUS Centralized Intermediate Repair Facilities

The second chapter examines the efficiency and effectiveness of CONUS Centralized Intermediate Repair Facilities to rapidly configure combat support and smoothly shift to sustainment in support of the AEF. With the use of CONUS CIRFs, there is a range of possible ANG participation in operating and managing CIRF facilities.

The CONUS CIRF analysis highlights several findings. First, small flying units with small intermediate-level maintenance (ILM) operations can be inefficient, which makes them a prime candidate for a transition to a CIRF. Economies of scale would suggest that one or at most a few large CIRFs for each commodity (for example, engines, pods, and avionics) might be the best option, potentially offering substantial cost savings without degrading weapon-system support. However, large CIRFs might be difficult for the ANG to staff from some local-area labor markets where trained technicians might not be available.

Second, transportation costs and transit times do not seem to significantly govern the CIRF location decisions. Therefore, for commodities for which adequate inventories are available, there is flexibility in the geographic location of the CIRF.

However, for commodities that do not have an inventory to support transit pipelines, the ability to consolidate ILM may be limited. In this case, large bases will be strong "mini-CIRF" candidates, providing home-station support as well as ILM for a few small units. These large bases generate a substantial portion of the demand for ILM. The ANG could negotiate with the active duty Air Force to staff all or a portion of these mini-CIRF maintenance complexes. The workload, supporting peacetime steady-state operations and then quickly shifting to contingency operations, would be well suited for a blended ANG/Air Force Reserve Command (AFRC)/active duty staffing rather than relying on civilian contractors. (See pp. 33–60.)

The Force Structure and Cost Estimating Tool— A Planning Extension to GUARDIAN

The third set of opportunities involves adding a new capability to GUARDIAN, the Force Structure and Cost Estimating Tool (FSCET), to develop enhanced program objective memorandum (POM) submissions based on actual weapon-system-usage factors or condition, including age and location history.

We found that the FSCET could be a useful extension of GUARDIAN. It provides an initial capability to examine an ANG fleet's airworthiness, operational suitability, availability, and operations and support (O&S) costs, allowing planners, analysts, and managers to evaluate the potential costs and effectiveness of alternative force-structure and combat-support resourcing plans before implementing them. Because the tool is script-driven and because fleets can be defined as needed by the using organization (for example, to the base level), the current FSCET data set and rules could be reconfigured to examine ANG-unique issues. At a minimum, the tool would also help the command estimate the consequences of the coming changes in force structure and operational tempo, thereby supporting the development of the command's inputs to the POM and the longer-range Air Force Capabilities Investment Strategy (AFCIS). (See pp. 61–95.)

Reachback Options

The fourth chapter examines the cost and effectiveness of using reachback,[3] in CONUS, to complete AOC tasks. Modified reachback capabilities for operational and combat support execution planning could reduce deployment requirements and the forward footprint.

During the reachback analyses, we found that the AOC augmentation arrangement currently being used (whereby personnel deploy forward and assist in work processes) is valuable. However, in moving specific tasks and services back to CONUS as ANG missions, ANG strengths are utilized and a place for deep knowledge and backup is developed. Reachback moves the ANG away from augmentation and into providing AOC capabilities from CONUS. This move may save on deployment and sustainment costs while requiring an initial investment in infrastructure to include communications and systems. Consolidation at one reachback location may offer some economies (for example, AOC-context information management expertise and information technology help), although not significant ones. There are, however, implications when moving to reachback. These new concepts could require a new concept of operations (CONOPS) and changes in the way the ANG operates (Title 32 state ANG personnel working Title 10 federal missions). (See pp. 97–132.)

Conclusions

These four Air Force mission areas were examined for possible engagement of the ANG. The objective was to leverage ANG strengths while mitigating their limitations. In each of these areas, there exists a range of potential ANG participation. A marginal cost analysis has been provided for each area (except for FSCET, for which cost would

---

[3] By *reachback*, we are referring to warfighters being located away from the area of operations—for example, operating unmanned aerial vehicles over Afghanistan and Iraq from within the continental United States.

be relatively small: The model has already been developed, and transfer to an ANG computer would likely involve little cost). Each of these areas could offer other potential opportunities of interest. The four areas evaluated were not meant to be exclusive (there are many other areas where the ANG could add value to the warfighter), but they are inclusive. The capability-based analysis approach that was used can be extended to identify other ANG capabilities.

Project AIR FORCE, at RAND, can work with the ANG to establish an analytic framework to guide internal transformation efforts. An approach similar to the approach taken during the Chief of Staff Logistics Review (CLR) (Lynch et al., 2004) could be used to identify opportunities for ANG transformation to better meet the AEF mission. RAND could help the ANG find tasks that can be accomplished to leverage ANG strengths while mitigating limitations.

Any transformational opportunity will require an ANG champion to develop the concept and negotiate mission requirements with the active duty Air Force. The ANG can choose from a range of options, such as those provided in this monograph. Each is likely to require negotiation with the active duty Air Force to determine the extent of participation.

As evidenced in this report, there are several new mission areas, such as CIRFs and AOC reachback, in which the ANG could help the Air Force achieve the operational effects necessary to enable the AEF.

Acknowledgments

Many persons inside and outside the Air National Guard provided valuable assistance for our work. We thank Lieutenant General Daniel James III, Director, Air National Guard, for supporting this analysis. We also thank Brigadier General David Brubaker, Deputy Director, Air National Guard, and Brigadier General Charles Ickes, Chief Operations Officer, Air National Guard, for their support of this effort.

We are especially grateful for the assistance given us by Air National Guard Director of Logistics Colonel Elliott Worcester and Deputy Director of Logistics Mr. Rich Rico. Both Colonel Worcester and Mr. Rico provided free and open access to their staffs during our analysis. Both were invaluable in providing points of contact both inside and outside the Air National Guard. We also thank Lieutenant Colonel Kevin Nuccitelli, ANG/XOXP, for his support during this study.

There are many people we would like to thank for their support of the civil engineering analysis in this report. We thank Colonel William Strandell, ANG/CE; Colonel Anthony Maida, ANG/CEX; and Mr. Bill Albro, ANG/CEP, from the Air National Guard. From Air Combat Command, we thank Brigadier General Patrick Burns, ACC/CE; Colonel (S) Edward Piekarczyk, ACC/CEX; Lieutenant Colonel Pamela Moxley, ACC/CEXO; and Ms. Nancy Balkus, ACC/CEX-2. We also thank Colonel Neil Kanno, AF/ILE, and Mr. Dick Pinto, AF/ILEXX, from the air staff.

For the CIRF analysis, we would like to thank the Reliability, Availability, Maintainability for Pods and Integrated Systems (RAMPOD) Office—in particular, Mr. James Bryan and Mr. Robbie Ricks. We would also like to thank the men and women of the 4th and 20th Component Maintenance Squadrons, especially Major Tom Miller and Major James Long. At Headquarters Air Combat Command (ACC), we thank Major Joseph Connell, Chief Master Sergeant Garza, Chief Master Sergeant Brunt, Major Chris Urdzik, and Master Sergeant Ty Elliott. We also thank Mr. Larry Williams from the ANG Bureau, Lieutenant Colonel Andy Bouck and Lieutenant Colonel Shawn Harrison from the Air Staff, and Captain James McKenna and the Air Force Logistics Management Agency (AFLMA) staff for all their support. We thank those bases that allowed us to tour their facilities: 1 FW, Langley AFB, Virginia; 4 FW, Seymour-Johnson AFB, North Carolina; 20 FW, Shaw AFB, South Carolina; 169 FW, McEntire ANGB (SC-ANG); 125 FW, Jacksonville International Airport (IAP) (FL-ANG); 138 FW, Tulsa IAP (OK-ANG); and 131 FW, Lambert–St. Louis IAP (MO-ANG).

We extend our appreciation to Colonel Mary Marshall, ANG/XPY; Lieutenant Colonel Mark Bower, ANG/XPYI; Lieutenant Colonel Timothy Tierney, ANG/XPYB; and Major William Rader, ANG/XPYA, from the Air National Guard for their support and interest in the GUARDIAN work at RAND.

For the reachback analysis, we thank Colonel Brock Strom, ANG/XO; Colonel Kathleen Fick, ANG/XOI; Major Patrick Cobb, ANG/XOI; Major Michael Norton, ANG/XOOC; Major Karl Stark, ANG/XOXE; Mr. David Robinson, ANG/C4B; and Senior Master Sergeant Michele Branch-Dorsey, ANG/XO, all from the National Guard Bureau. From the New York Air National Guard, we thank Colonel Tony Basile, 174 Fighter Wing Commander, and Colonel Joseph Bulmer, Commander, 152 Air Operations Group, and his staff, especially Lieutenant Colonel Chris Cahill and Lieutenant Colonel Howard Gordon. We also met with Brigadier General (S) Robert Knauff, NY-ANG Chief of Staff, to discuss issues from the state perspective. From the Missouri Air National Guard, we thank Colonel David Newman, Commander, 157 Air Operations Group and his staff. We also thank Lieutenant Colonel John Drake Selmer from the Air Force Command and Control and Intelligence, Surveillance, and Reconnaissance Center for his assistance in tracking down cost data. We thank Colonel Henry Haisch, AMC TACC/XON. At Beale Air Force Base, we thank Lieutenant Colonel Joseph DiNuovo, 548 Intelligence Group, for his support. We also thank Lieutenant Colonel Les Gonzalez, Commander, 152 Intelligence Squadron, Nevada Air National Guard, for spending many hours with us.

Finally, at RAND, we thank John Drew, Robert Kerchner, Gary Massey, and Bob Roll for their contributions and critiques of our work. We would especially like to thank John Ausink and Isaac Porche for their thorough reviews of this monograph, which helped shape this document into its final, improved form. We also thank Ben Van Roo for his contributions to the CIRF analysis. And, we thank Darlette Gayle and Angela Holmes for spending countless hours working on this project.

Abbreviations

ACC	Air Combat Command
ACS	agile combat support
AD	active duty
AEF	Air and Space Expeditionary Force
AETC	Air Education and Training Center
AF FVB	Air Force Fleet Viability Board
AFB	Air Force Base
AFCAIG	Air Force Cost Analysis Improvement Group
AFCIS	Air Force Capabilities Investment Strategy
AFI	Air Force Instruction
AF/IL	Deputy Chief of Staff for Installations and Logistics, U.S. Air Force
AFLMA	Air Force Logistics Management Agency
AFMC	Air Force Materiel Command
AFRC	Air Force Reserve Command
AFRES	Air Force Reserve
AFSC	Air Force specialty code
AFTOC	Air Force Total Operating Cost
ALC	Air Logistics Center
AMC	Air Mobility Command
AMD	Air Mobility Division

AMOCC	Air Mobility Operations and Control Center
ANG	Air National Guard
ANG/LG	Air National Guard Director of Logistics
AOC	Air and Space Operations Center
AOG	Air Operations Group
AOR	area of responsibility
APPG	Annual Planning and Programming Guidance
Apt	airport
ARC	Air Reserve Component
ARS	Air Reserve Station
ART	AEF UTC Reporting Tool
ASD	average sortie duration
ATO	air tasking order
AWM	awaiting maintenance
AWP	awaiting parts
BBS	Bare Base Set
BEAR	Basic Expeditionary Airfield Resources
BEEF	Base Engineer Emergency Force
BOS	base operating support
BSL	base stock level
C2	command and control
CAF	combat air forces
CAOC	Combined Air and Space Operations Center
CAS	close air support
CE	civil engineer
CEMS	Comprehensive Engine Management System
CER	cost-estimating relationship
CIRF	Centralized Intermediate Repair Facility
CLR	Chief of Staff Logistics Review

CMDB	Consolidated Manpower Database
COD	Combat Operations Division
COMAFFOR	Commander, Air Force forces
CONOPS	concept of operations
CONUS	continental United States
CORE	Cost Oriented Resource Estimating
CS	combat support
CSAR	combat search and rescue
CSC2	combat support execution planning and control
CSL	CONUS support location
csv	comma-separated value
DCGS	distributed common ground station
DIRMOBFOR	Director of Mobility Forces
DLR	depot-level repair
DMAG	Depot Maintenance Activity Group
DoD	Department of Defense
DO	director of operations
DOTMLP	doctrine, organization, training, materiel, leadership, and personnel
DPMP	Customer Service and Career Enhancement
DT	dynamic targeting
DTO	dynamic targeting officer
DWS	deployable MRC/steady state
DWX	deployable MRC
DXS	deployable steady state
EAF	Expeditionary Aerospace Force
ECS	expeditionary combat support
EOD	explosive ordnance disposal
ERT	engine rail team

EW	electronic warfare
FMC	fully mission capable
FOL	forward operating location
FSCET	Force Structure and Cost Estimating Tool
FSL	forward support location
FVB	Fleet Visibility Board
FY	fiscal year
FYDP	Future Years Defense Plan
GATM	Global Air Traffic Management
IAP	international airport
ILM	intermediate-level maintenance
IM	information management
IMA	individual mobilization augmentee
INT	in transit
INW	in work
ISDN	Integrated Services Data Network
ISR	intelligence, surveillance, and reconnaissance
ISRD	Intelligence Surveillance Reconnaissance Division
IT	information technology
IWS	information work space
JEIM	Jet Engine Intermediate Maintenance
JFACC	joint forces air component commander
JFC	joint force commander
JMC	Joint Movement Center
JOA	joint operations area
JointSTARS	Joint Surveillance and Target Attack Radar System
JTF NA	Joint Task Force Noble Anvil
JWC	Joint Warfare Center

LANTIRN	low-altitude navigation and targeting infrared for night
LCOM	Logistics Composite Model
LNO	liaison officer
LRU	line replaceable unit
MAF	mobility air forces
MAJCOM	major command
MC	mission capable
MCO	major contingency operation
MDS	mission design series
MENS	Mission Essential Needs Statement
MILP	Mixed-Integer Linear Program
MRC	monthly recurring cost
MTBF	mean time between failures
MTTR	mean time to repair
NAS	naval air station
NBC	nuclear, biological, and chemical
NGA	National Geospatial-Intelligence Agency
NORAD	North American Aerospace Defense Command
NORTHCOM	U.S. Northern Command
NRC	nonrecurring cost
NSA	National Security Agency
NSUTC	nonstandard unit type code
O&M	operations and maintenance
O&S	operations and support
OCONUS	outside the continental United States
ODO	offensive duty officer
OIF	Operation Iraqi Freedom

OIM	cost of maintenance labor that is kept available for wartime operations but that is unused (except for training) in peacetime
OOB	order of battle
PAA	primary aerospace vehicle authorization
PACAF	Pacific Air Force
PACAF/DO	Director of Operations, Pacific Air Forces
PAF	Project AIR FORCE
PB	President's Budget
PDM	programmed depot maintenance
PDMCAT	Programmed Depot Maintenance Capacity Assessment Tool
PDS	Air Force Program Data System
POL	petroleum, oil, and lubricants
POM	program objective memorandum
Prime BEEF	Priority Improved Management Effort Base Engineer Emergency Force
QDR	Quadrennial Defense Review
RAMPOD	Reliability, Availability, Maintainability for Pods and Integrated Systems
REMIS	Reliability & Maintainability Information System
RTU	readiness training unit
SA-ALC	San Antonio Air Logistics Center
SABLE	Systematic Approach to Better Long-Range Estimates
SAF/FM	Assistant Secretary of the Air Force, Financial Management and Comptroller
SCIF	Sensitive Compartmented Information Facility
SDDC	Military Surface Deployment and Distribution Command
SIDO	senior intelligence duty officer

SLEP	service life extension program
SODO	senior offensive duty officer
SPD	system program director
SPG	Strategic Planning Guidance
SPO	system program office
SRU	shop replaceable unit
START	Strategic Tool for the Analysis of Required Transportation
TACC	Tanker Airlift Control Center
TACP	tactical air control party
TAI	total active inventory
TCT	time-critical targeting
TDS	theater distribution system
telecon	teleconference
TST	time-sensitive target
UAV	unmanned aerial vehicle
UMD	unit manning document
USAFDC	U.S. Air Force Doctrine Center
USAFE	U.S. Air Forces, Europe
UTC	unit type code
UTE	utilization
VTC	videoteleconferencing
WMD	weapons of mass destruction
WRM	war reserve materiel
WMP	war and mobilization plan
WR-ALC	Warner-Robins Air Logistics Center
WRE	war reserve engine
WSCRS	Weapon System Cost Recovery System
WSS	weapon system security [personnel costs]

CHAPTER ONE

Introduction

The Air Force developed the Air and Space Expeditionary Force (AEF) concept so that a tailored, sustainable force could respond quickly, when appropriate, to national security interests. In conducting the research described in this monograph, we focused on the needs of the Air Force, as a whole, in achieving operational effects to enable the AEF. This analysis concentrates on transformation opportunities for better meeting combat support mission needs for the AEF. Using this view, we investigate the role that the Air National Guard (ANG) may play in these transformational opportunities that would capitalize on, or leverage, ANG strengths and provide effective and efficient approaches to achieving the desired operational effects, such as the ability to configure support rapidly and the ability to deploy and employ quickly.

VANGUARD, the new vision for the ANG, released in December 2002, calls for the ANG to consider, select, and implement new missions, new concepts, and new cultures that leverage ANG strengths and ensure that the ANG continues to add value as warfighters and to warfighters in the future. The Air National Guard, through the VANGUARD vision, has recognized the need to undertake a fundamental reexamination of its force-provider structure to ensure that it continues to play a leading role in meeting the AEF mission. VANGUARD unit concepts might include blending (mixing active duty and ANG personnel in the same unit), associate (assigning an active duty unit to an ANG base or vice versa), and other nonstandard approaches for meeting Total Force needs.

As evidenced by Operations Enduring Freedom and Iraqi Freedom, the active duty force alone cannot meet the demands of recent operational tempo. In this monograph, we evaluate how fundamentally different policies, at the unit level and above unit level, are likely to affect Total Force capabilities in meeting the needs of the evolving AEF mission. We then evaluate the effectiveness and efficiency of using the ANG in new ways to support the AEF.

The ANG possesses unique traits that can be strengths, including the following:

- Offering citizen soldiers who are patriotic volunteers
- Providing a skilled and experienced workforce
- Bringing community involvement and support for ANG personnel, personnel's spouse, and personnel's employer
- Furnishing the capacity to support large-scale contingencies or tailored unit type codes (UTCs)[1] to meet limited, time-specific needs
- Activating for a time period or to accomplish a mission
- Coming from/staying in a *civil* status for civil support missions.

Other aspects of the ANG can cause limitations to supporting a mission, such as the following:

- This workforce is primarily part-time; the part-time–full-time mix may be different for some transformational missions
- Limits are placed on the times for service call-up and duty tours
- As lengths of deployments extend, the number of volunteers to deploy may diminish
- Employer expectations and labor-market demographics may define recruiting markets.

---

[1] A *UTC* is a five-digit alphanumeric code assigned to a specific, predefined group of manpower and/or equipment units that provide a specific operational capability. For example, 4F9FP is the UTC that represents a Fire Protection Operations Team.

The goal of this analysis is to identify ways in which to support AEF operational goals that build on ANG strengths while mitigating their limitations.

Analytic Approach

We began by reviewing the new Department of Defense (DoD) Strategic Planning Guidance (SPG) (2004b) and the Quadrennial Defense Review (2004a). These documents outline the goals and the capabilities that have been identified for DoD to pursue in developing a program objective memorandum (POM). The documents also discuss a capabilities-based planning approach that each of the services should use to evaluate their ability to meet the scenario requirements outlined in the guidance.

The guidance specifies that capabilities will be created to (1) **one**, ensure homeland defense; (2) deter aggression in **four** major areas of the world, and engage in a number of small-scale contingencies if needed; (3) and if deterrence fails in the four areas of strategic importance, to be able to engage in **two** major contingency operations (MCOs) simultaneously; (4) with the ability to win **one** decisively while engaging in the other until the first is won, and then win the second MCO.

The Air Force Annual Planning and Programming Guidance (APPG) expands on how the Air Force will respond to the DoD SPG. The AEF concept of operations (CONOPS) specifies the operational effects that the Air Force is striving to achieve within the guidance received from the SPG and APPG. We also reviewed the changes being considered to Air Force operational-level organization—the critical role of the Commander, Air Force forces (COMAFFOR) in presenting forces to the combatant commander and the overlap of combat support authority and responsibility with joint force commanders and unified/joint staffs.

We derive the Total Force combat support and reachback[2] capabilities that are needed to support these operational effects. Finally, we develop ANG options, where appropriate. We determine the effectiveness and efficiency of ANG options in comparison with other options for delivering the needed capabilities, taking into consideration the strengths and limitations of the ANG.

ANG strengths are important to the Total Force capability. One aim of the research is to quantify these strengths and apply the values to current and/or evolving missions within an operational warfighter context. By following this analytic approach, we intend to show the most cost-effective opportunities for the ANG to contribute to the AEF mission from the perspective of the Total Force.

Background of the Agile Combat Support System

Earlier RAND studies present the framework for an agile combat support (ACS) system (comprising forward support locations, CONUS support locations, forward operating locations, and robust command and control capabilities) able to support the AEF concept (Tripp et al., 1999; Galway et al., 2000). In Table 1.1, we identify ACS capabilities that enable expeditionary operational effects, in the left-hand column, and some of the ACS concepts that are needed to enable those effects, in the right-hand column.

Transformational Opportunities Evaluated

Of the desired operational effects listed in Table 1.1, there were numerous transformational opportunities we could have evaluated. In this monograph, we concentrate on configuring combat support rapidly, deploying/employing quickly, and smoothly shifting to sustainment. Specifically, we evaluated the following four agile combat support capabilities:

---

[2] By *reachback*, we are referring to warfighters being located away from the area of operations—for example, operating unmanned aerial vehicles over Afghanistan and Iraq from within the continental United States.

Table 1.1
An ACS System Able to Support the AEF

Desired Operational Effect	Agile Combat Support Capability to Enable Effect
Foster an expeditionary mind-set	Combat support (CS) leaders who understand expeditionary operations Expeditionary mind-set instilled in combat support personnel Expeditionary scheduling rules
Configure support rapidly	Robust combat support execution planning and control (CSC2) capabilities • Estimate resource needs quickly • Tailor ACS network to scenario rapidly • Establish ACS control parameters for feasible plans • Track performance against control parameters • Modify processes as necessary Robust end-to-end distribution capabilities
Deploy/employ quickly	Rapid forward operating location (FOL) site-survey techniques Robust FOL development Attention on engagement policies and pre-surveys Leaned deployment packages and reduced deployed footprint Rapid deployment of non-unit resources (war reserve materiel [WRM])
Shift to sustainment smoothly	Enhanced forward support locations/CONUS support locations (FSLs/CSLs) linkages to resupply FOLs
Maintain readiness for operations in Defense Planning Scenarios	Resource planning factors that are aligned to reflect current rotational and contingency employment practices
Reduce combat support footprint	Exploit technology—communications, munitions, etc.

SOURCES: Tripp et al. (2000); Galway (2000); and Tripp et al. (1999).

• Civil engineering deployment and sustainment capabilities
• CONUS Centralized Intermediate Repair Facilities (CIRFs)

- The Force Structure and Cost Estimating Tool—A Planning Extension to GUARDIAN[3] capabilities
- Air and Space Operations Center (AOC) reachback missions.

Organization of This Monograph

Chapter Two examines new deployment concepts using modified UTCs in civil engineers (CE). By modifying some CE UTCs in the Establish the Base Force Module, short but intense CE tasks are completed in one UTC, then personnel are withdrawn. A second UTC, composed of fewer personnel, would be created to provide continued CE sustainment support. These concepts would reduce active component requirements while opening more opportunities for the ANG to accept CE tasks on a volunteer basis.

Chapter Three examines the efficiency and effectiveness of continental United States (CONUS) Centralized Intermediate Repair Facilities with ranges of ANG participation in operating and managing these facilities. By expanding CIRF capabilities, home-station and deployment requirements could be reduced.

Chapter Four involves adding a new capability to GUARDIAN, the Force Structure and Cost Estimating Tool (FSCET), to develop enhanced Program Objective Memorandum submissions based on the actual usage factors or condition, including age and location history, for a particular weapon system.

Chapter Five examines the cost and effectiveness of using reachback, in CONUS, to complete AOC tasks. Modified reachback capabilities for operational and combat support execution planning could reduce deployment requirements and forward footprint. Reachback could also tap endemic ANG force model strengths of mission knowledge, experience, civilian skills and experience, and continuity.

---

[3] GUARDIAN is an Air National Guard information system used to track and control the execution of plans and operations, such as funding and performance data.

These four mission areas were chosen to leverage ANG strengths and mitigate ANG limitations. The analysis of each opportunity follows a similar process: We first discuss the current Air Force practice, then the transformational concept. We then describe the specific analysis method used to evaluate alternative concepts and options in each area, then we compare the capabilities and costs of each alternative. Finally, we present ANG options for participation in each transformational area. We want to stress that each option will have a range of possible opportunities for the ANG to pursue in negotiations with the active Air Force.

Following the Conclusions, Chapter Six, we provide one appendix with information about the decision tree applied in Chapter Five.

CHAPTER TWO

Civil Engineering Deployment and Sustainment Capabilities

Two AEF operational effects—deploy or employ quickly and smoothly shift to sustainment—are greatly influenced by civil engineering processes. This chapter examines transformational deployment concepts associated with civil engineering and develops concepts for new sustainment capabilities. The examples will illustrate a range of options the Air Force and Air National Guard could choose to implement.

Current Expeditionary Combat Support Practice

First, we quantify the Air Force civil engineering deployment capability, subject to current and alternative policies. To quantify these capabilities, we use the current planning and deployment concept of Force Modules. Force Modules are sets of UTCs that define capabilities for creating and operating out of a deployed location. Five Force Modules have been developed: Open the Base, Establish the Base, Operate the Base, Provide Command and Control, and Generate the Mission. The timing of the arrival of one Force Module may overlap with that of another, but, in general, the first to deploy is the Open the Base module. This module is a lean set of UTCs largely consisting of air traffic control, security forces, and some materiel-handling equipment. Its purpose is to prepare the base to receive the other Force Modules. Our focus here will be on the Establish the Base Force Module, the one that contains most of the capability to set up the base infrastructure of housing (tents), medical facilities, food services, power generation, and so forth.

Although most Force Modules contain some civil engineering UTCs, the preponderance of civil engineering resources reside in the Establish the Base Force Module. In terms of manpower, the 213 UTCs that make up the Establish the Base function call for 565 persons, 178 of whom fall in civil engineering UTCs. Hence, civil engineering constitutes nearly a third of the manpower positions of this Force Module.

All of the following illustrative calculations will be in terms of how many bases can be established according to the prescription of this Force Module. We recognize that not all bases are alike. Depending on base population and infrastructure, the civil engineering UTCs that are required to "establish" a base may differ in type and number. The analytic methodology used in succeeding calculations can incorporate more-flexible, parameterized lists of UTCs required to set up and sustain a base. We will use the Establish the Base list of UTCs for simplicity, and because this list has been accepted by the Air Force for planning purposes.[1]

Each Establish the Base Force Module contains 26 civil engineering UTCs, of 15 different types (each type representing a different capability). These provide support in four areas: engineering craftsman, readiness, explosive ordnance disposal (EOD), and fire protection (see Figure 2.1). Engineering craftsman UTCs provide expertise in base erection, power distribution, water purification and distribution, excavation, and related areas. Readiness UTCs provide detection and decontamination for nonconventional weapons (nuclear, biological, and chemical). EOD UTCs provide base-clearance operations and the securing and disposal of unexploded ordnance. Fire protection UTCs provide protection against fire for both aircraft and structures throughout the base.

---

[1] For a methodology that captures the variations in deployment capabilities, see Snyder and Mills (2004).

Figure 2.1
Civil Engineering UTCs to Establish a Base

	UTC	Description	UTCs to establish a base	Persons in UTC
Engineering craftsman	4F9AP	Prime BEEF Power Pro Team	2	2
	4F9EA	Prime BEEF Team A	1	55
	4F9EP	Prime BEEF Team C	2	25
	XFBJ1	BBS Technical Supv. Team	1	13
	XFBJ3	BBS Erection Supv. Team	1	30
Readiness	4F9DA	NBC Team—Heavy	1	2
	4F9DB	NBC Team—Light	1	2
	4F9DC	NBC Team—Augmentation	3	2
EOD	4F9XA	EOD Management Team	1	2
	4F9X1	EOD Lead Team	1	6
	4F9X3	EOD Base Support Team	1	2
Fire protection	4F9FA	Fire Protection—Manager	1	1
	4F9FJ	Fire Protection—Incident Command Team	3	2
	4F9FN	Fire Protection—Mgmt. Augmentation	1	1
	4F9FP	Fire Protection Operations Team	6	6

SOURCES: U.S. Air Force, XOXW, Manpower and Equipment Force Packaging, February 2004; U.S. Air Force, XOA, Force Modules, February 2004.
NOTES: BBS = Bare Base Set; NBC = nuclear, biological, chemical; Prime BEEF = Priority Improved Management Effort Base Engineer Emergency Force.
RAND MG375-2.1

The fundamental engineering craftsmen units are called Priority Improved Management Effort Base Engineer Emergency Force (Prime BEEF) teams. The three principal teams are denoted by the letters A, B, and C. The three teams form modular deployment groups for initial beddown support and subsequent augmentation and follow-on support. Note that, as of May 2004, the frequently deployed Prime BEEF Team B (UTC 4F9EB) does not appear in the Establish the Base Force Module. Further, note that the Air Force Reserves (AFRES) posture their Prime BEEF A Team as a distinct UTC (4F9EW, in lieu of 4F9EA). The Reserves have created a distinct UTC because they prefer a 58-person team over the 55-person team used by the Guard and active duty personnel. UTC 4F9EW is not explicitly listed in the Force Modules, so counting the number of Prime BEEF A teams in the Force Modules excludes the 12 Air Force Reserve Prime BEEF A teams.

For simplicity, much of the following analyses will focus on a subset of the civil engineering UTCs in the Establish the Base Force Module, the engineering craftsman UTCs. These skills fall into the five UTC types listed in Figures 2.1 and 2.2. We are interested first in how many of each of these UTC types the Air Force has by component.

The Air Force postures individual UTCs against AEF requirements. Once postured, the database that so lists UTCs is the AEF Library. This library specifies how many of each UTC type exist, and, for each entry, considerable other data. Of those data, three are important for this analysis: the component responsible for that UTC, the priority for deployment (via a code), and in which AEF that UTC is assigned, or if the UTC is considered an enabler[2] (and thus not assigned to an AEF rotation). For example, of the UTCs of type 4F9EP, there are 89. Each of these 89 has a separate entry specifying the unit, a deployability code, and the AEF information. The deployability code is called the nonstandard UTC (NSUTC) and indicates whether that UTC is expected to deploy for normal rotations, for major-theater wars only, or is reserved for home-station requirements. The details of these codes are complex, and understanding these details is not necessary for this study. We will be considering only those UTCs coded DWS (deployable MRC/steady state) and DWX (deployable MRC), which are the sum of all those coded for full major-theater war deployments. The overwhelming majority of all civil engineering UTCs are included in these two codes.

Figure 2.2 summarizes these data from the AEF Library. It shows how many UTCs are needed for the Establish the Base function, how many persons are in each UTC, and how many of the

---

[2] An *enabler* is a high-demand/low-density capability that is not assigned to an individual AEF but can be shared across all AEFs, such as unmanned aerial vehicles.

UTCs are in each of the components. For example, looking at the 4F9AP UTC, we see two of these UTCs indicated in the Establish the Base Force Module, and each UTC requires 2 persons. The ANG has 175 of these UTCs, and hence 350 authorized manpower positions for this UTC type. All together, these civil engineering UTCs represent 10,667 authorized manpower positions, distributed among the components as follows:

- 4,821 active duty
- 5,130 ANG
- 716 AFRES (including the 4F9EW UTCs).

Figure 2.2
Current Posturing of Engineering Craftsman UTCs in Establish the Base Force Module

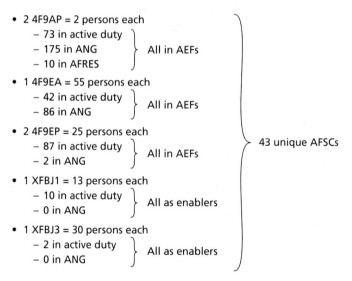

SOURCES: U.S. Air Force, XOXW and XOA, deployable MRC/steady state (DWS) and deployable MRC (DWX) nonstandard unit type codes (NSUTCs) in Cycle 4 AEF Libraries and Force Modules as of February 2004.
RAND *MG375-2.2*

Each of these UTC types specifies a specific skill level, called an Air Force specialty code (AFSC). Some of these AFSCs are common to more than one of the UTCs. When we explore alternative UTCs to perform this same mission, the number of unique AFSCs in these UTCs will become important. These five engineering craftsman UTCs specify 43 unique Air Force specialty codes.

Transformational Concept

In the current concept of opening and establishing a base, the forces deployed for the Open the Base role, called the contingency response group, deploy and set up their associated equipment, a minimal set of materiel that prepares the site to receive the other Force Modules. A contingency response group generally numbers around 100 persons. When the site is prepared, the substantially larger Establish the Base team arrives. When the Establish the Base team can take over the services of the smaller contingency response group, the latter group redeploys and is available to open another base. At this point, the Establish the Base team begins constructing the base infrastructure in preparation for the combat aircraft and all other personnel. However, when the teams to establish a base have built the base infrastructure and the site is ready to receive its combat forces, the Establish the Base teams remain in the same numbers to sustain the base. Hence, the same engineering craftsmen who initiate the beddown also do the day-to-day maintenance on the facility during its operation.

To examine possible ways in which civil engineering capabilities might be increased without changing the end strength or the ratio of ANG to active duty, we explore an alternative base-setup concept (Figure 2.3). In this transformational concept, a set of UTCs is deployed to perform the Establish the Base function, then is withdrawn, much like the contingency response group. The Establish the Base team is followed by a Sustainment UTC that is leaner than the sum of the Establish UTCs; nevertheless, it provides for adequate civil engineering sustainment capabilities. This concept would reduce the

Figure 2.3
Illustrative Reposturing of Engineering Craftsman UTCs

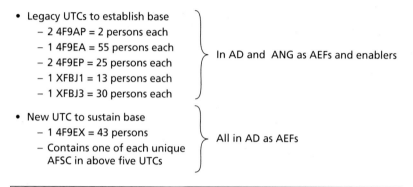

- Legacy UTCs to establish base
  - 2 4F9AP = 2 persons each
  - 1 4F9EA = 55 persons each
  - 2 4F9EP = 25 persons each   In AD and ANG as AEFs and enablers
  - 1 XFBJ1 = 13 persons each
  - 1 XFBJ3 = 30 persons each

- New UTC to sustain base
  - 1 4F9EX = 43 persons
  - Contains one of each unique   All in AD as AEFs
    AFSC in above five UTCs

Retain current force mix between AD and ANG and current total end strength

NOTE: AD = active duty Air Force.
RAND *MG375-2.3*

long-term commitment of civil engineering personnel at deployed locations and would provide a rotational role for establishing a base that could be filled in part by ANG personnel.

The exact constitution of these UTCs under the proposed transformation concept could be adjusted. Our purpose is to explore initially what benefits might accrue if Establish the Base UTCs could rotate to establish multiple bases, and if a leaner Sustainment UTC could relieve some airmen to establish additional bases. For illustrative purposes, we examine a hypothetical Sustainment UTC that contains one each of every unique AFSC in all of the engineering craftsman UTCs in the Establish the Base Force Module. We call this new Sustainment UTC 4F9EX. The Establish the Base function is assumed to require precisely the UTCs specified in the Establish the Base Force Module. The new Sustainment UTC is created by shifting manpower positions from the existing UTCs.

Analytic Approach

For each expeditionary combat support (ECS) UTC concept, we evaluate several cases. We analyze how many bare bases can be established within an AEF pair without an ARC call-up. We also evaluate how many bare bases can be established with an AEF pair with different Air Force Reserve Component call-ups. In each case, we evaluate how much capability an ARC call-up provides within an AEF pair, in contrast to calling forward capabilities in another AEF pair. We also investigate what a rational split of the new UTCs would be between ANG and active duty personnel. Through the analysis, we found that, in each case, several factors drive the results:

- Deployment duration rules for ANG/active duty
- Time to establish a bare base
- Total end strength in engineering craftsman UTCs
- Mobilization status.

To quantify deployment capabilities, requirements for the deployment capability must be compared to available or authorized resources in light of deployment policies. For the following illustrative calculations, we use the Establish the Base Force Module to define the requirements, and compare these requirements to the resources listed in the Cycle 4[3] AEF Libraries.

The approach can be altered to accept alternative requirements and resources. For example, the more-parameterized requirement model Strategic Tool for the Analysis of Required Transportation (START) (Snyder and Mills, 2004) could be used to define requirements for establishing a base that vary with base population and level of threat to which the base is exposed, both conventional and nonconventional. Also, note that the AEF Libraries indicate the *authorized* manpower positions; they do not reflect the *available* re-

---

[3] The Air Force divided its capability into ten equal buckets, called AEF rotations. Those rotations are paired into five AEF cycles. Cycle 4 consists of the UTCs associated with AEF 7 and 8, listed in the AEF Library.

sources. The latter can be estimated by using resource data from the AEF UTC Reporting Tool (ART).

We will examine deployment capabilities given a number of alternative deployment policies. For AEF policies, we follow the policies for Cycle 4. We estimate the capability if every airman in a UTC assigned to an AEF serves for one 90-day period each cycle (of 15 months), and if each airman assigned to one of the two AEF enablers (A or B) serves one 180-day period each year. The results give an average capability for a pair of the 10 AEFs and an average of the A and B enablers.

We also explore Air Reserve Component (ARC) mobilization policies. One fraction of the ARC serves as active duty (we call this the fraction called up), and the other serves for a user-defined period per year (we call this the service time of the ARC fraction not called up). Figure 2.4 is a schematic of the methodology used in this analysis.

Baseline Analysis

For the baseline analysis, we examine how many bases can be established as a function of percentage of ARC personnel called up to serve in an active duty capacity.

Figure 2.4
Methodology for Establish the Base Capability Assessments

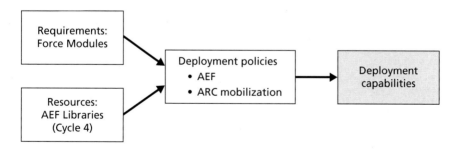

RAND *MG375-2.4*

Figure 2.5 shows the deployment capabilities for establishing a bare base in the civil engineering functional area. The requirements are those specified by the Establish the Base Force Module. Each bar indicates the capability to establish bases for the indicated UTC, given the numbers of those UTCs in the AEF Library. The divisions within the bars in Figure 2.5 indicate what fraction of that capability resides in the active duty, the ANG, and the AFRES component. The results show the capability defined by an average AEF pair with none of the ARC called up.

If one of a particular UTC is needed to establish a base (according to the requirements prescribed in the Force Module), and two of those UTCs are listed as available in the AEF Library for an AEF pair, then two bases can be established concurrently. So, even

Figure 2.5
Baseline Case of Civil Engineering Capability to Establish a Base, Zero-Percent ARC Call-Up

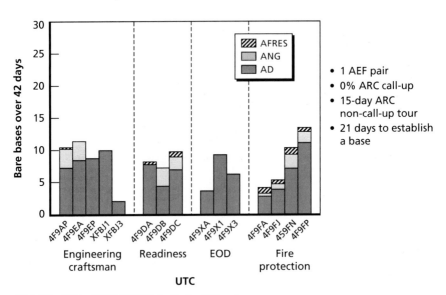

SOURCE: DWS + DWX NSUTCs in Cycle 4 Libraries.

RAND MG375-2.5

though it is assumed (for argument) that it takes one team 21 days to perform the Establish the Base mission, it is possible that more than two bases can be established during the 42-day period if multiple teams are available to work concurrently. This concurrency is a key factor in this analysis, and it recurs in all the ensuing figures in this chapter.

Related and in addition to this concurrency is the concept of rotation. Two of the UTCs (XFBJ1 and XFBJ3) are assumed to be able to rotate out once a base is established and, hence, be available to establish other bases. For these UTCs, the capability represents what they could do over a 42-day period if each team can establish a base every 21 days. We explore below the implications if other UTCs can rotate similarly to these UTCs. All of the parameters listed along the right-hand side of the figure will be examined in subsequent examples.

The results of this baseline analysis show that the AEF Library has imbalances in the number of UTCs relative to those needed for establishing a bare base. For instance, the XFBJ3 personnel are the limiting resource in this UTC. As shown in Figure 2.5, the XFBJ3 skills limit the number of bases that can be established during the 42 days to two bases. The figure also shows an apparent overabundance of firefighters, 4F9FP, in the UTC, more than necessary. This type of information can be used to adjust resources in UTCs such that all are in balance with the most limiting resource type. We emphasize, however, that these personnel have other functions beyond their roles in the Establish the Base Force Module, such as augmentation to an established base. Setting the optimal mix of UTCs requires examining all these roles, not just the Establish the Base mission.

Figure 2.6 reports the same capabilities as in the preceding figure, except that 50 percent of the ARC are now assumed to be called up, serving as active duty; the other half serve for 15 days per year.

Note that the capabilities of those UTCs that contain ARC personnel have greatly increased relative to those in Figure 2.5 and that the proportion of capabilities of those UTCs due to the ARC is also much increased.

Figure 2.6
Baseline Case of Civil Engineering Capability to Establish a Base, 50-Percent ARC Call-Up

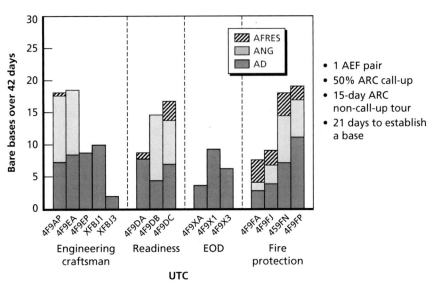

SOURCE: DWS + DWX NSUTCs in Cycle 4 Libraries.
RAND MG375-2.6

The remainder of this chapter explores alternative deployment policies, as well as the consequences of assigning skilled personnel to alternative UTCs. In all of these calculations, the number of personnel in the active duty and ANG components will remain fixed, but they will be redistributed among the UTC types in order to attain optimal and equivalent capability across all UTCs. Hence, personnel will be shifted among the UTCs so that each UTC for establishing a base will have the same capability, and the Sustainment UTC will have sufficient numbers to sustain all the bases established by the Establish the Base UTCs.

In these preliminary calculations, AFRES UTCs are ignored.

Analysis with No ARC Call-Up

The first analysis set focuses on no ARC call-up. We examine how many bases can be established as a function of time.

Figures 2.7, 2.8, and 2.9 show the Establish the Base engineering craftsman capability per AEF pair as a function of time. We assumed that no ARC is called-up and that all ARC personnel serve for 15 days per year. We further assumed that a single team requires 21 days to establish a base and that more than one base can be established in a 21-day period if multiple teams can work concurrently. Figure 2.7 shows the capability over 30 days. Figure 2.8 shows the same results over 60 days, and Figure 2.9, over 90 days.

Each bar gives the capability for the indicated UTC, and patterns/shadings within each bar display how much of the capability resides in the active duty and in the ANG. The left-hand bar gives the capability based on the current UTC posturing and deployment policies. This is a baseline for comparison. The right-hand bar gives the

Figure 2.7
Engineering Craftsman Capabilities to Establish a Bare Base over 30 Days

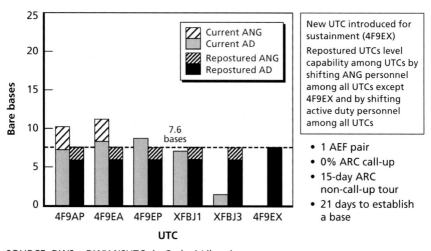

SOURCE: DWS + DWX NSUTCs in Cycle 4 Libraries.
RAND *MG375-2.7*

Figure 2.8
Engineering Craftsman Capabilities to Establish a Bare Base over 60 Days

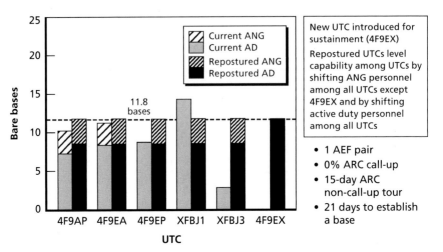

SOURCE: DWS + DWX NSUTCs in Cycle 4 Libraries.
RAND *MG375-2.8*

Figure 2.9
Engineering Craftsman Capabilities to Establish a Bare Base over 90 Days

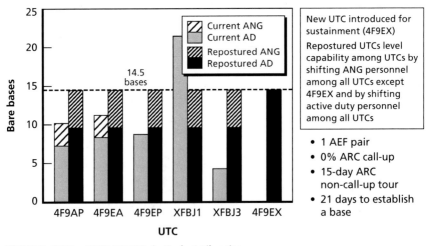

SOURCE: DWS + DWX NSUTCs in Cycle 4 Libraries.
RAND *MG375-2.9*

capability if a new UTC (4F9EX) is introduced for sustainment (as detailed in Figure 2.3), and the personnel are re-distributed among all the UTCs shown in order to give an equivalent capability.

Figure 2.10 summarizes the data of Figures 2.7 through 2.9, with the additional information of what capability could be generated out of the current UTCs and deployment policies if the personnel were redistributed to achieve equivalent capabilities for all the UTCs.

The left-hand bar for each UTC gives the current capability for the UTC based on its current posturing and deployment policies. This bar is the same as the left-hand bar on the preceding three figures.

The middle bar for each UTC gives the capability for the UTC if personnel are redistributed, but no Sustainment UTC is introduced.

The right-hand bar for each UTC gives the capability for the UTC if personnel are redistributed and a Sustainment UTC is

Figure 2.10
Comparison of Current Posturing, Rebalanced Posturing, and Posturing Rebalanced with New UTC

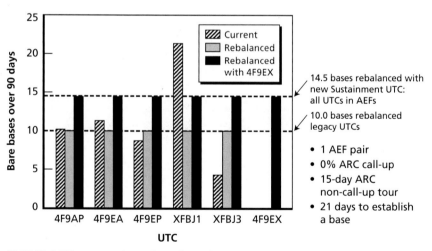

SOURCE: DWS + DWX NSUTCs in Cycle 4 Libraries.
RAND MG375-2.10

introduced. This bar is the same, conceptually, as the right-hand bar in the preceding three figures.

The middle and right-hand bars allow comparison of the current policy and the Sustainment UTC policy on equivalent terms. Note that, for the parameters used (no ARC call-up, 15-day service per year for the ARC, and 21 days for a team to establish a base), introduction of the Sustainment UTC increases the capability to establish bases by 45 percent over 90 days.

Analysis with 50-Percent ARC Call-Up

This second analysis set is similar to the first, except that 50 percent of the ARC are now called up.

The next three figures show the Establish the Base engineering craftsman capability per AEF pair as a function of time. It is assumed that 50 percent of the ARC are called up to serve as active duty personnel and that the remaining 50 percent of the ARC personnel serve for 15 days per year. Each team is assumed to take 21 days to establish a base. Figure 2.11 shows the capability of concurrent teams over 30 days. Figures 2.12 and 2.13 show the same results over 60 and 90 days, respectively.

Each bar gives the capability for the indicated UTC, and patterns and shadings within each bar display how much of the capability resides in the active duty and the ANG components. The left-hand bar gives the capability based on the current UTC posturing and deployment policies. This is a baseline for comparison. The right-hand bar gives the capability if a new UTC (4F9EX) is introduced for Sustainment, and the personnel are redistributed among all the UTCs shown in order to give an equivalent capability.

Figure 2.11
Engineering Craftsman Capabilities to Establish a Bare Base over 30 Days, 50-Percent ARC Call-Up

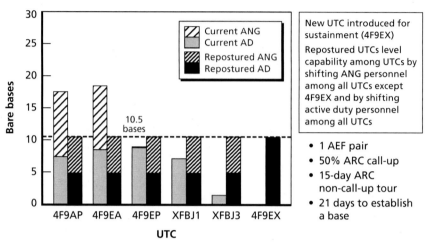

SOURCE: DWS + DWX NSUTCs in Cycle 4 Libraries.
RAND *MG375-2.11*

Figure 2.12
Engineering Craftsman Capabilities to Establish a Bare Base over 60 Days, 50-Percent ARC Call-Up

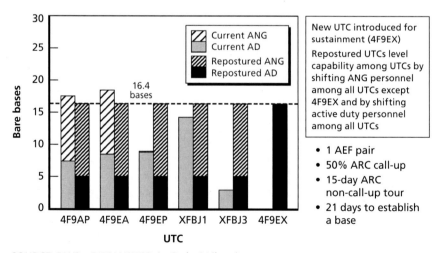

SOURCE: DWS + DWX NSUTCs in Cycle 4 Libraries.
RAND *MG375-2.12*

Figure 2.13
Engineering Craftsman Capabilities to Establish a Bare Base over 90 Days, 50-Percent ARC Call-Up

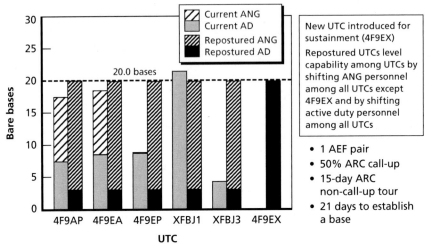

SOURCE: DWS + DWX NSUTCs in Cycle 4 Libraries.
RAND MG375-2.13

Figure 2.14 summarizes the data of Figures 2.11 through 2.13, with the additional information of what capability could be generated out of the current UTCs and deployment policies if the personnel were redistributed to achieve equivalent capabilities for all the UTC types.

The left-hand bar for each UTC gives the current capability for the UTC based on its current posturing and deployment policies. This bar is the same as the left-hand bar in the preceding three figures.

The middle bar for each UTC gives the capability for the UTC if personnel are optimally redistributed but no Sustainment UTC is introduced.

The right-hand bar for each UTC gives the capability for the UTC if personnel are redistributed and a Sustainment UTC is introduced. This bar is the same, conceptually, as the rightmost bar in the preceding three figures.

Figure 2.14
Comparison of Current Posturing, Rebalanced Posturing, and Posturing Rebalanced with New UTC—50-Percent ARC Call-Up

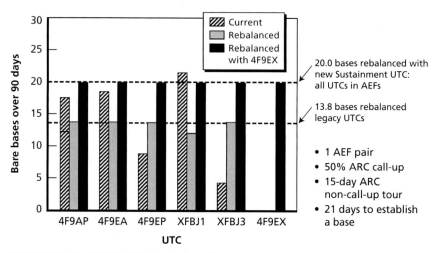

SOURCE: DWS + DWX NSUTCs in Cycle 4 Libraries.
RAND *MG375-2.14*

The middle and right-hand bars allow comparison of the current policy and the Sustainment UTC policy on equivalent terms. Note that, for the parameters used (50 percent ARC call-up, 15-day service per year for the remainder of the ARC, and 21 days for each team to establish a base), introduction of the Sustainment UTC increases the capability to establish bases by 45 percent over 90 days.

Figure 2.15 summarizes the results of the first and second analysis sets. Plotted is the number of bases that can be established as a function of time.

The dashed curves indicate the capability of the current UTCs, given a redistribution of personnel in order to achieve equivalent capability with each UTC. These curves summarize the data of the middle bars in Figures 2.10 and 2.14. The lower curve is for no ARC call-up; the upper curve is for 50-percent ARC call-up.

Figure 2.15
Summary of Analyses as a Function of Time

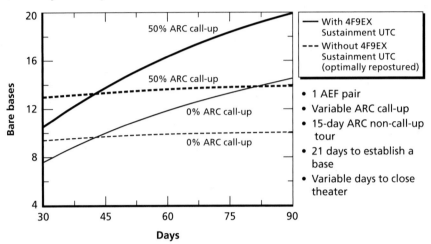

SOURCE: DWS + DWX NSUTCs in Cycle 4 Libraries.
RAND MG375-2.15

The solid curves indicate the capability if a new Sustainment UTC is created. These curves summarize the data of the rightmost bars in Figures 2.10 and 2.14. Like the leftmost bars in Figures 2.10 and 2.14, the lower solid curve is for no ARC call-up; the upper curve is for 50-percent ARC call-up.

Note that, for periods longer than about 45 days, the introduction of the Sustainment UTC gives significantly more capability relative to the current policies.

Cost Analysis

Next, we examine deployment, sustainment, and redeployment costs associated with these analyses. We also attempt to identify associated effects on infrastructure costs.

The current requirement for engineering craftsmen to open a base is 152 personnel in skilled trades—construction specialists, electricians, and plumbers. Once the base is open, those personnel remain at the deployed location for the duration of the deployment. Our alternative proposed process would establish a new Sustain the Base capability consisting of 43 personnel and would build a new Open the Base capability.

Because the initial deployment would be the same amount of people and equipment, the deployment cost and redeployment cost are the same with either the current process or the proposed transformational process. Those costs can be estimated by multiplying the per-hour airlift cost ($56 per hour per person[4]) by the number of flying hours to the deployment location (20 hours each way, 40 hours total), by the number of personnel deploying (152), by the number of AEF rotations in a year (4), or approximately $1.4 million per year.

We estimated sustainment cost by multiplying the number of people deployed, by the number of days deployed, by the number of deployments, by $30.[5] In Sustainment, the two processes have very different costs (see Table 2.1). The current practice would call for 152 personnel times 90 days times 4 AEF rotations per year times $30, or approximately $1.6 million. The transformation concept would call for 125 personnel times 21 days times $30, plus 43 personnel times 90 days times 4 AEF rotations times $30, or $543,000.

In the transformational concept, if the 125 redeploy before all of the forces deploy, there could also be a savings for tents. Assuming the deploying force could reuse a tent that the initial CE craftsmen put up, the savings could be a reduction in tent purchases of approximately $1.3 million.[6]

---

[4] We calculated the cost by taking the cost of a commercial 747 ($18,648 per hour) and dividing it by the number of passengers it can carry (335), which yields approximately $56 per person per hour.

[5] The $30 is an accepted Air Force planning factor that includes the costs of food, laundry, per diem for incidentals, combat pay, and some cost of security.

[6] These calculations are based on one Basic Expeditionary Airfield Resources (BEAR) 550f set costing $5.624 million and providing tents for 550 persons.

Table 2.1
Estimated Annual Sustainment Costs

	Current Practice	Transformational Concept
Personnel	152	125
Length of deployment	90 days	21 days + 43 personnel at 90 days
AEF rotations	4	0 + 43 personnel at 4 rotations
Cost	$1.6 million	$543,000

Totaling, the new transformational sustainment costs would save approximately $1 million per year, with a $1.3-million cost avoidance for tent purchases. Assuming a consistent rate of deployment and a tent life span of five years, we obtained an overall savings over ten years of approximately $12.6 million.

Introduction of a New Sustainment UTC

Figure 2.16 shows the effect of the introduction of a Sustainment UTC as a function of the time it takes to establish a base, all other factors being equal. As in Figure 2.15, the dashed curve gives the capability of the current UTCs, given a redistribution of personnel in order to achieve equivalent capability with each UTC. The solid curve gives the capability if a Sustainment UTC is introduced. Note that the Sustainment UTC gives significantly more capability, unless it takes a team of engineering craftsmen, on average, more than six weeks to establish a base.

Figure 2.16
Engineering Craftsman Capabilities to Establish a Bare Base over 90 Days as a Function of Time to Establish a Base

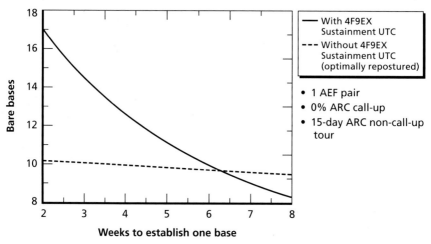

SOURCE: DWS + DWX NSUTCs in Cycle 4 Libraries.
RAND MG375-2.16

Air Force and ANG Civil Engineer Deployment and Sustainment Implications

In completing this analysis, we found that converting some UTCs and changing their deployment concepts might better support the AEF missions than current concepts do. Specifically, the ANG 4F9AP and 4F9EA UTCs could be converted to other 4F9EP, XFBJ1, and XFBJ3 UTCs. The deployment concept of these UTCs might be changed to support short, intense periods of work—lasting two to three weeks. Then, once a base is established, the UTCs might be extracted. These changes may be better able to support the AEF mission than current concepts do.

The creation of a Sustainment engineering craftsman UTC and ANG acceptance of more Establish the Base responsibilities could reduce active deployment requirements, as well as deployment and sustainment costs. New ANG UTCs could serve as modules of homeland defense first responder units. Although not evaluated here, the creation of a Close the Base Force Module could offer additional opportunities to reduce active component deployments. Further, the concepts used in this analysis may be applicable to other UTCs in other fields.

CHAPTER THREE

Continental United States Centralized Intermediate Repair Facilities

CONUS Centralized Intermediate Repair Facilities (CIRFs) enable rapidly configured combat support and a smooth shift to sustainment—two desired operational effects of the AEF. This chapter discusses the current and transformational concepts associated with CONUS CIRFs. Its objective is to evaluate the effectiveness and efficiency of the CONUS CIRF concept and to offer specific recommendations for its potential implementation, focusing on the role of the Air National Guard in that implementation. We present a sample analysis for the TF-34 engine to illustrate a range of options that the Air Force and Air National Guard could choose to implement.

Current Intermediate-Level Maintenance Practice

The Air Force employs a three-level maintenance concept—organizational, intermediate, and depot levels—for the following four commodities:

- fighter aircraft (F-15, F-16, and A-10) engines, including the TF-34, F-100, and F-110 families
- low-altitude navigation and targeting infrared for night (LANTIRN) pods
- electronic warfare (EW) pods
- F-15 avionics.

Organizational-level maintenance involves refueling, arming, and conducting pre- and postflight inspections and diagnostics, along with performing on-equipment maintenance. These repairs are performed through the removal and replacement of line replaceable units (LRUs), which are complete assemblies that are installed directly onto the aircraft. Organizational maintenance is performed at (or near) the flight line. *Intermediate-level maintenance* (ILM) involves the repair of such major aircraft subcomponents as engines and avionics LRUs that have been removed from the aircraft. An ILM shop can repair such a component through work on the component itself, and through the removal and replacement of subcomponents (shop replaceable units [SRUs]). An ILM shop cannot repair failed SRUs, however. *Depot-level maintenance* involves both complete overhaul of major components and repair of SRUs. Depot-level maintenance is performed at a single centralized site for each commodity.

Current Air Force practice calls for operating units to perform their own intermediate-level maintenance at a backshop[1] that is collocated on the base with the operating unit. While such a structure promotes self-sufficiency (especially during deployed operations), it results in a large number of small and potentially inefficient maintenance operations. For example, the TF-34 engine is supported at nine different ILM facilities, with many of these facilities supporting single-squadron ANG units. As a result, many of these ILM resources may be underutilized.

Transformational Concept

Previous RAND research (Peltz et al., 2000; Feinberg et al., 2001; Amouzegar, Galway, and Geller, 2002) has examined the costs and benefits of CIRFs, wherein ILM is consolidated into a small number of relatively large facilities, focusing on the support of AEF-deployed operations outside CONUS (OCONUS). These studies found that

---

[1] Each air base establishes ILM facilities, or *backshops,* which are authorized to repair LRUs through the removal and replacement of failed SRUs or by other repair processes.

the CIRF concept enables expeditionary operations through an increased efficiency and reduction in deployed footprint, because the ILM shop is not deployed with the unit to the forward operating location (FOL). This allows for deployment time frames to be reduced, although it requires a dedicated transport commitment to ship broken commodities from the FOLs to the CIRF and serviceable commodities from the CIRF to the FOLs. It should be noted that ILM is designed to support sustainment operations. Spares inventories—for example, war reserve engines (WREs)—are intended to support the surge operations associated with the early days of a deployment. Thus, the CIRF workload is likely to be relatively stable and have steady workloads.

Although these studies considered CONUS CIRFs, the focus was not on the application of the CIRF concept to home-station operations within CONUS. Additionally, it should be noted that these studies did not explicitly consider the unique characteristics of ANG and Air Force Reserve (AFRES) units. The expeditionary mind-set remains the primary focus (because CONUS-based units are the forces that deploy to support the AEF structure); however, other objectives must be considered when evaluating the ILM structure for CONUS units. CONUS CIRFs may afford increases in maintenance utilizations, through potential reductions both in cost and in the maintenance manpower requirement. The impact on the maintenance manpower requirement is of special interest, because CONUS CIRFs may lead to a reduction in manpower requirements for stressed Air Force specialty codes (AFSCs). We emphasize, however, that any increases in efficiency through the implementation of CONUS CIRFs must not come at the cost of a reduction in capabilities: Support of AEF operations remains the most important goal.

Analytic Approach

The objective of this analysis is to evaluate the effectiveness and efficiency of potential CONUS ILM concepts, and to offer specific recommendations for the future ILM structure. Here, we present a

CONUS CIRF analysis associated with one commodity, the TF-34 engine, and discuss the implications of centralized ILM that are of key interest to the ANG.[2]

The following questions are addressed in this study:

- How many CONUS CIRFs are needed? For some commodities, a single CONUS CIRF may be able to provide acceptable ILM support. Other commodities may require a set of regional "mini-CIRFs," providing home-station support as well as ILM for a few small units. For certain high-value, high-repair-rate items, home-station repair may remain the preferred option.
- Where should each of these CIRFs be located? Home-station bases provide one set of candidate CIRF locations. Collocation with Air Force Materiel Command (AFMC) depots may be another possibility. Commercial sites, located near major civilian transport hubs, may also offer benefits, which warrants their inclusion on the list of candidate locations.
- How large should each CIRF be? In addition to a list of suggested CONUS CIRF locations, each operating unit's ILM must be assigned to a CIRF. Each CIRF must then be sized, in terms of manpower and equipment, to support the demand associated with it.

An important consideration that is not addressed in this monograph is, Who should operate each CIRF? It should not be assumed that a CIRF located at, for example, an AFRES base would necessarily be operated by AFRES. A CIRF may potentially be operated by active duty, AFRES, ANG, DoD civilian, or private-contractor personnel, or any combination of the above. This analysis was performed

---

[2] Analyses for all potential CIRF commodities (fighter aircraft engines, LANTIRN pods, EW pods, and F-15 avionics) are in unpublished RAND research by James M. Masters, Ronald G. McGarvey, Louis Luangkesorn, Stephen Sheehy, John G. Drew, Robert Kerchner, Ben Van Roo, Robert S. Tripp, and Charles Robert Roll, Jr. A detailed presentation of the technical aspects of the mathematical models used in this analysis is given in unpublished RAND research by Ronald G. McGarvey, James M. Masters, Louis Luangkesorn, and Ben Van Roo.

using maintenance manpower standards; it did not examine differences in capabilities between, for example, active duty and ANG maintenance personnel.

The analysis supporting these questions will address a wide range of CONUS CIRF considerations. However, the factors that are expected to have the greatest influence upon the solutions include the following:

- *Extent of economies of scale in the maintenance operation.* One way to achieve economies of scale is through the increased utilization of small and inefficient operations. For certain commodities, additional economies of scale may be realized through the consolidation of several smaller operations into one large facility.
- *Number of spares available to support the new pipelines.* If ILM repair is moved away from the operating unit's home station, spare commodities would be necessary to support the transport pipelines. For commodities with abundant spares, these transport pipelines will not be a constraining factor. However, for commodities with a short supply of spares, the transport pipelines associated with a CIRF structure may prove prohibitive, if additional spares cannot be purchased to fill the added pipeline. It is important to note, however, that in addition to transport pipelines, operating units' spares requirements also must support *repair time,* which comprises in-work (INW), awaiting-maintenance (AWM), and awaiting-parts (AWP) times. Our analyses assume that, although the ILM structure will have no effect on either the INW or AWP times,[3] it will have a significant effect upon AWM time. Generally speaking, queueing effects and workload distribution act in such a way that AWM

---

[3] ILM structure may affect AWP times, depending upon the root cause of AWP. If AWP times exist because of a systemwide shortage of components, the ILM structure should have no effect. However, if AWP times exist due to uneven demand across the large set of ILM facilities, consolidation of ILM should decrease AWP through pooling of stock and smoothing of demand variance. Note that savings in AWM may outweigh transit costs, resulting in a net increase in serviceable spares under a centralized structure.

time decreases as maintenance is consolidated into a smaller number of larger facilities.

- *Transportation, implementation/changeover, and personnel costs.* The trade-offs between the various cost components will also influence the solutions. A more centralized solution should achieve savings through economies of scale in operating and personnel costs, although it will also incur additional transportation and CIRF implementation/changeover costs.

- *Differences in personnel costs and capabilities.* The CIRF manning will be determined from a potential pool of active duty, AFRES, ANG, DoD civilian, and private-contractor personnel. The differing costs and capabilities (for example, availability and performance) of each personnel type[4] will greatly influence the CIRF recommendations.

The research outcomes associated with developing options for the design of the affected CONUS CIRF network are determined by the numerous data and scenarios that are used to evaluate the options. In terms of scenarios, more than only the peacetime flying schedule for these CONUS units are considered in this analysis. The integration of the CONUS CIRF into OCONUS support for AEF deployments must also be analyzed.

Figure 3.1 presents the modeling framework used to evaluate CONUS CIRF network design options.[5] The three uppermost boxes present major categories of the model's requirements for input data:

- *Mission requirements* include the scenarios to be supported, peacetime-training requirements, and potential contingency re-

---

[4] See Chapter Two for a description of UTC taxonomy and personnel calculations.

[5] More information about the modeling framework and analyses of other potential CIRF commodities (fighter aircraft engines, LANTIRN pods, EW pods, and F-15 avionics) is in unpublished RAND research by James M. Masters, Ronald G. McGarvey, Louis Luangkesorn, Stephen Sheehy, John G. Drew, Robert Kerchner, Ben Van Roo, Robert S. Tripp, and Charles Robert Roll, Jr.

quirements. These scenarios drive the CIRF demand requirements.

- *Asset pools* include the commodities to be supported (engines,
  pods, and avionics LRUs) and the repair equipment (including
  test stations, engine rails, hush houses,[6] etc.)
- *Rates, factors, and costs* include the commodity failure and repair
  rates, repair-equipment availability factors, transportation costs
  and times, personnel costs, facility operating and construction
  costs, etc.

Figure 3.1
CONUS CIRF Modeling Framework

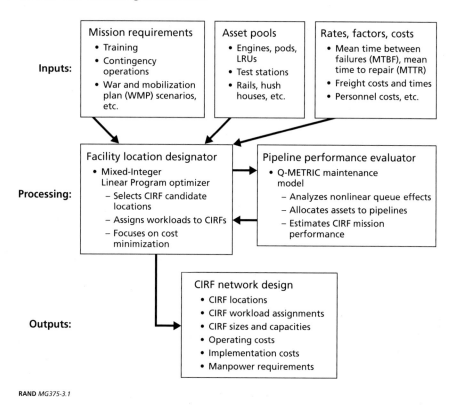

---

[6] A *hush house* is an engine test facility that suppresses engine-testing noise.

Our analytic framework combines a Mixed-Integer Linear Program (MILP) with a newly developed stochastic inventory model, called Q-METRIC.[7] This framework explicitly considers the combinatorially large number of potential network designs (including both assignment of bases to ILM facilities and the sizing of ILM facilities). The two boxes in the middle of the figure represent the mathematical models:

- *Facility Location Designator,* a Mixed-Integer Linear Program optimizer, designs a CIRF network by selecting CIRF locations from a candidate list, assigning workload to the CIRFs, and determining CIRF manning and maintenance capacity. The mathematical objective of the MILP model is to minimize total system costs (including transport costs, operating costs, CIRF implementation and changeover costs, and personnel costs), subject to constraints on the available assets (both commodities and repair capabilities), along with constraints on system performance (for example, mission capable rates or expected back orders). Piecewise linear functions are used to provide good approximations of the nonlinear inventory and queueing effects.
- *Pipeline Performance Evaluator,* a modified version of the METRIC maintenance model (Sherbrooke, 1966, p. 55), is used to evaluate the performance of the CIRF network (in terms of number of serviceable spares commodities) determined by the Facility Location Designator. A key shortcoming of the METRIC approach to pipeline evaluation is its assumption of unconstrained maintenance capacity. When designing a CIRF network, the sizing of each CIRF is of great importance. Therefore, "Q-METRIC," an improved METRIC formulation, has been developed to explicitly consider the queueing (AWM) effects associated with finite maintenance capability.[8] Q-

---

[7] Unpublished RAND research by Ronald G. McGarvey, James M. Masters, Louis Luangkesorn, and Ben Van Roo on the technical aspects of the mathematical models used in this analysis.

[8] This work is an extension of Sleptchenko, van der Heijden, and van Harten (2002).

METRIC analyzes the nonlinear queueing effects associated with stochastic failure and repair, and it performs an allocation of spare assets to pipelines in a near-optimal fashion.[9]

The two mathematical models presented above operate iteratively, with the MILP determining a minimum-cost CIRF network and Q-METRIC evaluating the performance of that network. Initially, the MILP is solved with no constraint on system performance. The weapon-system support (measured using mission capable rates or number of serviceable spares) of the output CIRF network is then evaluated using Q-METRIC. A constraint is then added to the MILP requiring a slightly improved system performance, the new optimization model is solved, and Q-METRIC is used again to evaluate the new solution. This iteration is repeated until no further improvements can be made to the system performance.

The box at the bottom of Figure 3.1 represents the output from this mathematical model: a set of CIRF network designs, each containing a set of CIRF locations, the workload assignments from the bases to the CIRFs, the CIRF sizes and capacities, the operating costs, the implementation costs, and manpower usage, along with the dollar and manpower savings as compared to the current ILM policy.

In many commercial sectors—specifically, in production operations—transportation and facility costs often act in different directions when examining the number of facilities to establish to serve a given market. This relationship is shown in Figure 3.2. The *y*-axis shows annual operating costs, composed of transportation and facility-operating costs. As the number of facilities increases, the transportation costs decrease because the greater number of storage/

---

[9] METRIC models allocated inventory in a near-optimal fashion using marginal analysis, because it is time-prohibitive to perform the complete enumeration necessary to determine the optimal allocation.

Figure 3.2
In Commercial Practice, Opposing Cost Effects Often Suggest a "Cost-Optimal" Number of Locations

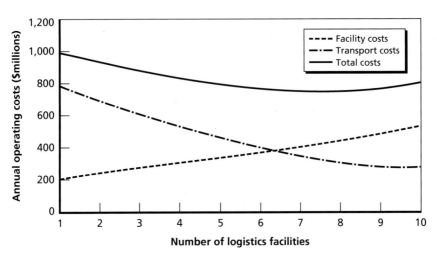

production facilities allows facilities to be situated closer to their markets. On the other hand, facility-operating costs increase with the number of facilities. The result is the familiar bathtub, or U-shaped, combined-cost curve that shows an optimal cost solution.

Unfortunately, such commercial facility-location analyses are typically modeled without explicitly accounting for the level of system performance. For this study, we emphasize that any increases in efficiency achieved through the implementation of CONUS CIRFs must not come at the cost of a reduction in capabilities (measured here as mission capable rates or serviceable spare levels). Supporting AEF operations and the warfighter remains the most important goal.

In this analysis, the goal is to identify the CONUS CIRF postures that provide the maximum system performance for the minimum total cost. As expenditures are reduced, weapon-system availability is necessarily degraded. The modeling framework presented in Figure 3.1 provides a means for determining the extent of these trade-offs. In practice, because of the economy-of-scale savings available via centralization of maintenance, the minimum-cost CONUS CIRF networks will have a small number of highly utilized facilities. System performance can be improved through increased manpower (which reduces the time that commodities spend in a queue) and through the use of additional repair facilities (which reduces the time that commodities spend in transit, although it detracts from economy-of-scale savings).

The set of solutions (that is, the set of CIRF network designs) resulting from the iterative procedure of Figure 3.1 is examined to determine the set of solutions residing on the *efficient frontier* (see Figure 3.3), wherein solutions appearing on the curve provide the highest level of weapon-system support available for a given level of expenditures. Each point lying on the efficient frontier represents a candidate CIRF network solution. Solutions appearing below the curve provide suboptimal performance for any expenditure level; the region above the curve does not contain any feasible solutions. This efficient frontier demonstrates the explicit trade-offs between system cost and system performance.

Figure 3.3
CIRF Network Trade-Off Options

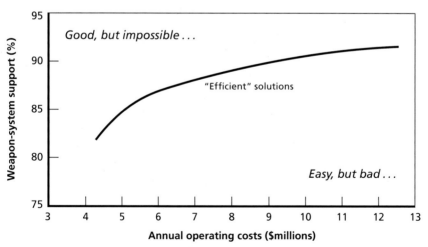

Preliminary Analysis of the TF-34 Engine

An examination of the Jet Engine Intermediate Maintenance (JEIM) structure for the TF-34 engine is presented here as an example of this CONUS CIRF analysis. This engine is used in the A-10, two engines per aircraft. Currently, 13 CONUS flying units use this engine (RAND-generated spreadsheet on CIRF OOB [order of battle], 2004). Some CIRF structure already exists for TF-34 ILM. Barksdale Air Reserve Station (ARS), Louisiana, is a CIRF for three Air Force Reserve units. Davis-Monthan AFB, Arizona, provides the ILM support for Nellis AFB, Nevada. Shaw AFB, South Carolina, which does not have an A-10 flying unit, provides a CIRF for Pope AFB, North Carolina; Eglin AFB, Florida; and Spangdahlem AB, Germany (Spangdahlem engines must be supported within the CONUS JEIM structure). The current CONUS (plus Spangdahlem) inventory is 106 spare engines.[10] The current total CONUS (plus Spangdahlem) war reserve engine (WRE) authorization is 42 engines (RAND, CIRF OOB spreadsheet, 2004).

The current manning at these units, obtained from unit manning documents (UMDs)[11] (U.S. Air Force, Customer Service and Career Enhancements [DMDP], 2003), was determined to be 311 full-time personnel, with 270 part-time drill personnel[12] in the Air National Guard and Air Force Reserves. Note that some of these drill personnel are also counted within the 311 full-time personnel. To estimate current costs, we assumed an annual cost of $60,000 per

---

[10] These data are from the RAND Corporation spreadsheet CIRF OOB (2004). They do not include the 11 additional engines authorized to Barksdale ARS, Louisiana, for its CIRF operation supporting the Air Force Reserve units at Whiteman and New Orleans. However, the conclusions presented in this chapter would remain unchanged if the 11 Barksdale engines were included.

[11] These documents are part of the Consolidated Manpower Database (CMDB), a product of the Air Force Manpower Data System, the system the Air Force uses to manage manpower requirements and authorizations.

[12] Traditional ANG personnel, who serve one weekend a month and two weeks a year, are often referred to as *drill personnel*.

full-time person and $15,000 per drill person, giving a current annual manning cost of $22.7M.

Figure 3.4 presents a map of the units currently using the TF-34 engine. Note that the point representing Shaw AFB in South Carolina indicates a current CIRF location that does not have a flying unit. Similarly, the point representing Dover AFB in Delaware indicates the aerial port of debarkation for those engines arriving from Spangdahlem. Currently, these engines are flown via Air Mobility Command into Dover and shipped via air-ride truck from Dover to Shaw AFB. For the purposes of this study, we assume that these

Figure 3.4
TF-34 Operating Locations

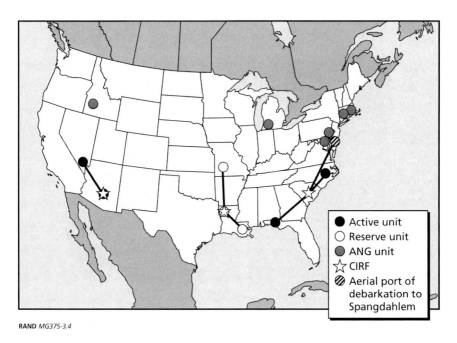

RAND *MG375-3.4*

engines emanate from Dover and ignore the transit cost from Germany to Delaware.

Table 3.1 presents further detail on the network of TF-34 bases.

To examine the potential for economies-of-scale savings in TF-34 JEIM operations,[13] we performed a Logistics Composite Model (LCOM) simulation analysis. LCOM is a statistical simulation model used by the Air Force to estimate the manning required for maintenance tasks.[14] We determined the maintenance manpower for varying numbers of primary aerospace vehicle authorizations (PAAs), presented in Figure 3.5. Note that this graph appears nonlinear in manning with respect to the PAA supported, indicating economies of scale. Note that at the leftmost end of the curve, roughly 30 JEIM

Table 3.1
Current TF-34 Network

Base Name	MAJCOM	PAA
Davis-Monthan AFB	ACC	66
Nellis AFB	ACC	11
Pope AFB	ACC	42
Spangdahlem AB (Dover AFB)	USAFE	18
Eglin AFB	AFMC	2
Martin State Apt	ANG	15
Barnes Apt	ANG	15
Boise Apt	ANG	15
Bradley IAP	ANG	15
W. K. Kellogg Apt	ANG	15
Willow Grove ARS	ANG	15
Barksdale AFB	AFRES	15
NAS New Orleans	AFRES	15
Whiteman AFB	AFRES	15

SOURCE: RAND Corporation, CIRF OOB spreadsheet (2004).
NOTES: Apt = Airport; ACC = Air Combat Command; MAJCOM = major command; PAA = primary aerospace vehicle authorization; USAFE = U.S. Air Forces, Europe; NAS = naval air station.

---

[13] Figure 3.5 presents results obtained from U.S. Air Force, Air Combat Command (1998). RAND staff produced similar LCOM analyses for the other commodities of interest.

[14] For a detailed discussion of the LCOM model, including its uses and limitations, see Dahlman (2002).

Figure 3.5
TF-34 LCOM Analysis

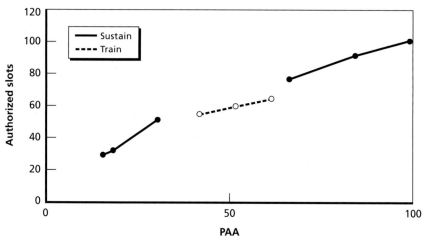

SOURCE: Results are from U.S. Air Force, Air Combat Command (1998). RAND staff produced similar LCOM analyses for the other commodities of interest.
RAND *MG375-3.5*

personnel are required to support 15 PAA (two men per PAA), whereas at the rightmost end of the curve, 100 JEIM personnel are required to support 100 PAA (one man per PAA). This is likely because of minimal crew size requirements (for example, an activity that requires a crew of five personnel, but which only utilizes the fifth person for one task). Additional economies of scale may again be possible through the improved utilization of small units' manpower.

The CIRF transit times were obtained using the DoD Standard Transit Time—Truckload (U.S. Department of Defense, Military Surface Deployment and Distribution Command [SDDC], 2004), and these times ranged from 1 to 7 days. An additional two days were added to each transit leg to allow for transit-preparation time. The transport costs were obtained from the CIRF CONOPS Transportation Computation Chart (Headquarters U.S. Air Force, 2004), assuming an air-ride trailer is used for each shipment.

TF-34 engines are inducted into the JEIM shop as a result of failures; their scheduled maintenance is performed at the Oklahoma City Air Logistics Center depot. TF-34 failures are generally expressed in terms of a mean time between failures (MTBF), which is a function of engine operating hours. The Air Force Propulsion Requirements System's MTBF estimate is 851 hours per removal.[15] An engine-induction rate into the JEIM shop is based on the assumed aircraft flying schedule. We posited a monthly utilization (UTE) rate (number of sorties per PAA per month) of 20, and an average sortie duration (ASD) of 1.5 hours per sortie. Thus, the monthly engine failure rate at a base was equal to 2*PAA*20*1.5/851; using a conversion of 365 days per 12 months gives a mean daily failure rate, summed across all CONUS engines, of 0.635. However, CONUS JEIM shops are assumed to operate 5 days per week; thus, the daily JEIM induction rate is equal to 7/5 times this failure rate, giving an overall mean of 0.889 JEIM induction per working day.

Engine-repair times are another critical piece of data. The Comprehensive Engine Management System (CEMS) database is the centralized Air Force standard system used for engine management. An analysis of CEMS data suggested a mean INW time of 385 hours for TF-34 engines,[16] with an attempt made to exclude time reported as INW when an engine is "in the system" but not being actively worked on—for example, overnight or on weekends.

The modeling of the JEIM presents another challenge. The JEIM repair procedure can be viewed as occurring in two stages. An *engine rail team* (ERT) performs engine repair. Following repair, every engine is sent to a *test cell,* where the repaired engine is tested to ensure that it is now serviceable. If the engine passes the test at the test cell, it goes back into the serviceable spares pool. If the engine fails the test at the test cell, it is returned to the ERT for further repair. Our mathematical modeling provides an accurate representation of this two-stage process, with ERTs and test cells modeled independently. The TF-34 engine spends an average of 16 hours per

---

[15] Actuarial Removal Interval Worksheet, Propulsion Requirements System FY2005, obtained from HQ AFMC/MSG/SLW.

[16] CEMS database; data collection from September 2001 through December 2003.

test at the test cell, and the test-cell reject rate is 12 percent.[17] Since an engine that fails at the test cell will have to undergo at least one more test, it can be determined that an engine spends an average of 18.2 hours at the test cell for each induction into the JEIM. The INW times obtained through the CEMS database do not differentiate between time at the ERT and time at the test cell. Thus, each engine spends an average of 385 − 18.2 = 366.8 hours at the ERT per induction into the JEIM.

The CIRF manning was computed in terms of ERTs and "test cell personnel." Each ERT was assumed to require a four-man crew, and the initial ERT at a repair location required an additional five personnel to repair engine accessories and small gas turbines. Each test cell was assumed to require a three-man crew. The CIRF was assumed to operate 16 hours per day, 5 days per week, requiring two 8-hour shifts per crew. Standard Air Force availability factors were used to compute an availability rate of 0.963. Finally, an additional 10-percent manning was assumed to account for supervisory and support personnel. Recall that significant economies of scale were evident from the LCOM simulation analysis, partly because one test cell can support many ERTs. Again, for this preliminary analysis, no differentiation was studied between different types of manpower.

The operating cost was assumed to be equal to the associated personnel cost, using a factor of $60,000 per man-year. The only CIRF setup cost considered was the cost required to obtain an additional test cell. It was assumed that the required T-9 test cells could be obtained from bases losing their JEIM. However, a building would need to be constructed to house the test cell, along with an augmentor/deflector repack kit and fire suppression, at a total cost of $3.9 million. These test cells require a major maintenance action every five years, costing between $500,000 and $1 million. Thus, the test-cell purchase was discounted over a five-year interval at a real discount

---

[17] ACC/LGMP, 2004.

rate of 2.1 percent,[18] resulting in an annualized cost of $1 million per CIRF test cell.

It was assumed that any base that performs only its own home-station repair would use its existing test-cell capabilities and would not incur this test-cell-setup cost. However, for any base that acts as a CIRF, the assumption was that this CIRF would not operate under the command of the local operating unit, which would need its own test cell (or hush house) for testing installed engines. Therefore, any CIRF would need to pay the test-cell-setup cost. The only exception was the current CIRF arrangement at Shaw, which was assumed to have one test cell available for CIRF operations at no cost. No constraint was assumed on the number of ERTs available, since engine rails are rather inexpensive, compared with their associated manning costs.

Figure 3.6 presents the results of our preliminary analysis of the TF-34 ILM structure, demonstrating the trade-off between annual cost (transport cost, plus operating cost, plus annualized test-cell-setup cost) and the number of serviceable spares available. Note that the *efficient frontier* curve actually represents a very large number of potential solutions: For any point of interest along this curve (for example, 71 serviceable spares at a cost of $30 million), an associated CIRF network design has been identified. Recall that the current CONUS (plus Spangdahlem) inventory is 106 spare engines, with a total CONUS WRE authorization of 42 engines.[19] All the potential solutions along the efficient frontier are well above the CONUS WRE requirement. Data obtained from the Oklahoma City Air Logistics Center (OC-ALC) indicate an average AWP of 9.25 percent of Base Stock Level spare engines (worldwide), over the period January through December 2003.[20] It was assumed that the JEIM

---

[18] Office of Management and Budget, White House, 2004. See http://www.whitehouse .gov/omb/circulars/a094/a94_appx-c.html.

[19] RAND Corporation, CIRF OOB, 2004.

[20] C. R. McIntosh, TF-34 briefing, OC-ALC/LR, 2004.

Figure 3.6
TF-34 CIRF Network Options—100 Percent in CONUS

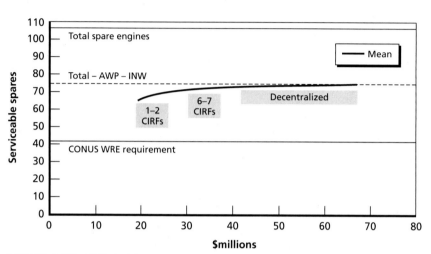

SOURCE: RAND CIRF models.
RAND *MG375-3.6*

structure would have no effect on the AWP rate. Multiplying this AWP value by the CONUS-wide spare pool of 106 engines gives a mean expectation of 9.8 AWP engines. These 9.8 engines were subtracted from the total pool of 106 spares, leaving a maximum pool of 96.2 serviceable spares. It was also assumed that the JEIM structure would have no effect on the INW engines. Given the assumed failure and repair rates, a mean of 21.4 engines is expected INW, yielding a maximum possible mean serviceable spare value of 74.8 engines (assuming zero engines AWM and zero engines in transit between the bases and JEIMs).

However, a CONUS CIRF must be able to support deployed operations as well. Thus, we examined a situation in which 20 percent of the units of interest are deployed. Instead of selecting individual units to deploy, we assumed that 20 percent of the PAA aircraft deployed from each unit, accounting for 54 A-10 aircraft. While this is somewhat unrealistic, it is necessary to avoid considering every possible deployment scenario. It was assumed that the 54 aircraft that deployed would have their TF-34 ILM performed at an OCONUS

CIRF, which would be staffed entirely by deploying personnel from the CONUS CIRFs. The 54 A-10s were assumed to be deployed to three different locations, each with 18 aircraft. In all instances, we assumed a 15-day one-way transit time to the OCONUS CIRF.[21] Note that OCONUS transit was not costed in this study, nor were the test cells required at the OCONUS CIRF. The AWP fraction was increased proportionally to the increase in the number of failures due to the deployed flying schedule. The CONUS WRE requirement was reduced by 20 percent to reflect the 20 percent of the PAA already deployed.

An aircraft flying schedule is again necessary to obtain an engine-induction rate into the OCONUS JEIM shop. We posited a monthly UTE rate of 30 sorties per PAA, with an average sortie duration of 3.0 hours per sortie (see Figure 3.7). The OCONUS CIRF was assumed to operate 24 hours per day, 7 days per week. A 60-hour workweek was assumed. Also, standard Air Force availability factors were used to compute an OCONUS availability fraction of 0.958. Observe that even for an indefinite deployment of 20 percent of the PAA, the serviceable spares level can be kept far above the WRE requirement.

We next tested a situation in which the same 20-percent deployment occurred, but with no OCONUS CIRF support. A 25-day one-way transit time to any CONUS CIRF was assumed. Also, it was assumed that the CONUS CIRF would maintain its 16-hours-per-day, 5-days-per-week work schedule (see Figure 3.8).

Note that the curve indicating the efficient frontier for the "all CONUS repair" scenario remains at or below the CONUS WRE requirement, regardless of the expenditures. This is because of the large

---

[21] We deliberately used an exceedingly conservative OCONUS transit time to demonstrate the supportability of the TF-34 in a CIRF framework. During the USAFE CIRF test, average one-way transit times of 5 or 6 days were observed for the F-100 and F-100 engines (TF-34 engines were not tested; see U.S. Air Force, 2002a).

Figure 3.7
TF-34 CIRF Network Options—20 Percent Deployed to OCONUS

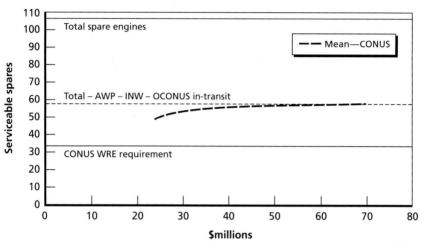

SOURCE: RAND CIRF models.
RAND MG375-3.7

Figure 3.8
TF-34 CIRF Network Options—20 Percent OCONUS, All CONUS Repair

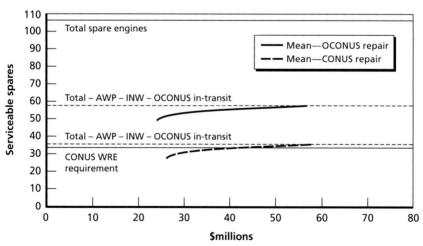

SOURCE: RAND CIRF models.
RAND MG375-3.8

number of engines in transit between OCONUS operating locations and CONUS. On average, 26.7 engines are in this 50-day-round-trip pipeline, ignoring the time spent at the CIRF. If this 25-day one-way transit time to CONUS could be reduced to, for example, 15 days each way, an additional 10.7 engines would be added to the serviceable spares pool. Another potential means for increasing the serviceable spares levels would be to increase the workweek at the CONUS CIRFs to a 24-hour, 7-day operation.

A similar analysis was performed for a 40-percent deployment, defined as two separate deployments identical to those described above. Assuming that two separate OCONUS CIRFs were to be used for the OCONUS JEIM repair, one CIRF supporting each deployment, we obtained the results in Figure 3.9. As observed previously, even for an indefinite deployment of 40 percent of the PAA, the serviceable-spares level can be kept far above the WRE requirement.

Figure 3.9
TF-34 CIRF Network Options—40 Percent Deployed to OCONUS

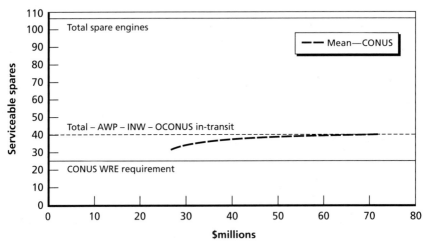

SOURCE: RAND CIRF models.
RAND *MG375-3.9*

We next tested a situation in which the same 40-percent deployment occurred, but with no OCONUS CIRF support. We assumed a 25-day one-way transit time to any CONUS CIRF and that the CONUS CIRF would maintain its 16-hour-per-day, 5-days-per-week work schedule. The results of this analysis appear in Figure 3.10.

The curve indicating the efficient frontier for the "all CONUS repair" scenario remains below zero engines, regardless of the expenditures, and would result in grounded aircraft because of insufficient serviceable engines. This result is, again, due to the large number of engines in transit between OCONUS operating locations and

Figure 3.10
TF-34 CIRF Network Options—40 Percent Deployed to OCONUS,
All CONUS Repair

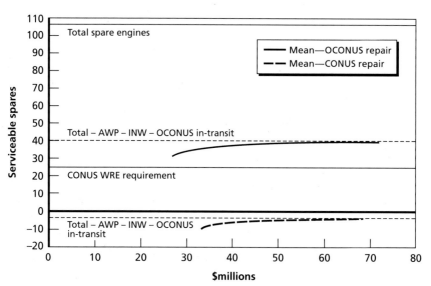

SOURCE: RAND CIRF models.
RAND *MG375-3.10*

CONUS. On average, 53.4 engines are in this 50-day-round-trip pipeline, ignoring the time spent at the CIRF. If this 25-day one-way transit time to the CONUS could be reduced to, for example, 15 days each way, an additional 21.4 engines would be added to the serviceable spares pool, which is still significantly below the CONUS WRE requirement. Another potential means for increasing the serviceable spares levels would be to increase the workweek at the CONUS CIRFs to a 24-hour, 7-day operation.

Cost Analysis

The *efficient frontier* curves presented in Figures 3.6 through 3.10 represent a very large number of potential solutions. Each point lying on these curves is associated with a specific CIRF network design. For illustrative purposes, we will examine the most-centralized solution obtained in this analysis: a single CONUS CIRF established at Shaw AFB for each deployment scenario. Table 3.2 summarizes the maintenance, transportation, and equipment (annualized test-cell-setup) costs, as well as the system performance and manpower implications associated with this single-CIRF solution.

For the 100-percent CONUS nondeployment case (first column of Table 3.2), a total manning of 295 is able to achieve a mean serviceable spares level of 65.4 engines, at an annual cost of $19.4 million. The maintenance manning portion of the cost equals $17.7 million, and the annual transport cost is only $685,000 to ship all TF-34 maintenance actions to Shaw. A second test cell was needed at an additional cost of $1.0 million.

These results can be compared against current ILM performance. Recall that current manning was determined to be 311 full-time personnel, and 270 drill personnel in the Air National Guard and Air Force Reserves. The mean annual transit cost associated with the current CIRFs at Barksdale ARS, Davis-Monthan AFB, and Shaw AFB

Table 3.2
Cost Comparison of TF-34 CIRFs

	100% CONUS	80% CONUS	60% CONUS
CIRFs	1	2	3
		(1 OC)	(2 OC)
Serviceable spares	65.4	49.2	31.6
Maintenance ($M)	17.7	22.5	26.3
Transportation ($M)	0.7	0.5	0.4
Equipment ($M)	1.0	1.0	0.0
Total ($M)	19.4	24.1	26.7
Total manning	295	375	438
		(130 OC)	(260 OC)

SOURCE: The manning data are from the RAND model, calibrated against LCOM outputs. Because of pipeline considerations, LCOM was not used directly.
NOTE: OC = OCONUS.

is $91,000. Adding this value to the annual manning cost computed earlier gives a current annual cost of $22.8 million.

However, these results compute only the personnel needed for peacetime training operations. Thus, a more fair comparison can be made against the current full-time manning, ignoring the drill positions, which are intended for deployments. This comparison gives a current annual cost of $18.7 million. Data obtained from the Oklahoma City Air Logistics Center indicate that the average serviceable spares pool was equal to 57.6 percent of the authorized base stock level (BSL), over the period January 2003 through December 2004.[22] Applying this rate to the CONUS BSL of 106 engines, we observe an estimated mean serviceable spares level of 61.1 engines. Thus, the current system has slightly larger manning than our one-CIRF solution (311 full-time versus 295). The current system has a slightly smaller total annual cost (roughly $1 million), owing to a lesser transport cost, and an avoidance of the test-cell-setup cost. However, current practice achieves only 61.1 mean serviceable spare engines, instead of the 65.4 engines for the one-CIRF solution. Of course, it should be noted that the WRE requirement for the TF-34 engines under consideration is only 42 engines. Thus, it appears that accept-

----

[22] C. R. McIntosh, TF-34 briefing, OC-ALC/LR, 2004.

able performance can be achieved through either solution, if only peacetime training operations are considered.

We now evaluate the 80-percent CONUS, 20-percent OCONUS costs and manpower requirements (second column of Table 3.2). The OCONUS CIRF requires total manning of 130, with an additional 245 personnel required at the Shaw CIRF, for a total manning of 375. This solution attains a total serviceable spares mean value of 49.2 engines, at an annual cost of $24.1 million.

For the 60-percent CONUS, 40-percent OCONUS options, each OCONUS CIRF requires total manning of 130, with an additional 178 personnel required at the Shaw CIRF for the aircraft remaining in the CONUS. Therefore, total manning is 438. This solution attains a total serviceable spares mean value of 31.6 engines, at an annual cost of $26.7 million.

These results indicate that acceptable performance can be achieved through a small number (likely, 1 or 2) of CIRFs. However, OCONUS CIRFs likely need to be operated to attain acceptable performance for extended deployment scenarios.

Air Force and ANG CIRF Implications

Several implications for the ANG result from this analysis. Overall, CIRFs offer the potential for cost savings, depending on the solution option selected, with no degradation in weapon-system support. Because ILM activities can exhibit economies of scale,

- small PAA flying units can be relatively inefficient in their ability to perform ILM
- small-workload units are likely candidates to be assigned to CONUS CIRFs
- scaled economies that persist at high levels of aggregation would lead to one or, at most, a few large CIRFs for each commodity (given pipeline assets), potentially offering substantial cost savings without degrading weapon-system support.

Second, variations in transport cost and transit time seem unlikely to significantly affect the CIRF-location decisions. Therefore, when there is adequate inventory to support peacetime transport pipelines associated with CIRFs, as is the case with the TF-34 engine, there is likely to be good flexibility in the geographic choice of CIRFs. It is likely that CIRFs could then be placed where a good workforce is located, at little detriment to performance. A potential complication is that large CIRFs might be difficult for the ANG to staff from a local community labor market.

For some commodities with high acquisition costs and high failure rates, the ability to consolidate ILM will be limited by asset inventories that cannot support the transit pipeline needed for CIRF operations. For these commodities, "large" bases will be strong "mini-CIRF" candidates, providing home-station support as well as ILM for a few small units. These large bases generate a large portion of the demand for ILM. In addition, for these types of commodities, we expect the solution to have network designs with small transit pipelines. For these types of commodities, the ANG could opt to negotiate with the active duty force to staff all or a portion of these mini-CIRF maintenance complexes, which would likely be located at large active duty bases.

The CONUS CIRF structure will need to move from supporting peacetime steady-state operations to supporting contingency operations smoothly and rapidly. Therefore, CONUS CIRF CONOPS will need to include the manpower and equipment requirements for augmenting OCONUS CIRFs and/or flying units during deployed contingency operations. As a result, this type of workload would be well suited for a blended ANG/AFRES/active duty staffing rather than relying on civilian contractors.

During peacetime operations, CONUS CIRF workloads will likely be relatively stable and have steady workloads. As a result, a blended CIRF unit with active duty, full-time ANG, traditional Guardsmen, and AFRES personnel might work well. The full-time ANG can provide a stable expertise base and facilitate training. Active duty personnel could provide a rotating pool of experienced technicians that could then deploy to bases or CIRFs as needs arise.

Traditional Guardsmen and AFRES personnel can provide deployment augmentees when needed.

CHAPTER FOUR

The Force Structure and Cost Estimating Tool— A Planning Extension to GUARDIAN

The Air National Guard designed GUARDIAN, a strategic resource management system, to monitor the execution of the Air National Guard's resource allocation process to ensure that individual units are receiving the needed resources and developing the intended capabilities for their contributions to the AEF's combat capabilities. The Air Force uses GUARDIAN to track and control execution of combat support resource plans and operations, including tracking funding and performance data. In this chapter, we discuss the current and transformational concepts associated with GUARDIAN, focusing mainly on how GUARDIAN could be extended to better estimate ANG resource requirements in the formulation of the POM and budgeting process submissions, according to actual weapon-system-usage factors or conditions, including age and location history. We envision adding a new capability to GUARDIAN, the Force Structure and Cost Estimating Tool (FSCET), that would enable planners, analysts, and managers to evaluate the potential costs and effectiveness of alternative force structure and combat support resourcing plans before implementing those plans.

The Use of Current GUARDIAN Capabilities

Current GUARDIAN capabilities focus mainly on ensuring that an existing plan for force structure and combat support system design and resource allocation is implemented faithfully and effectively. That is, it takes the current funding and other resource plans as a given and monitors the delivery and use of those resources to ensure that the ANG's readiness, sustainment, and training goals are achieved. When those goals are not achieved or new operational requirements emerge, the ANG takes corrective action: Sometimes it reallocates resources within the current fiscal year to rectify a critical near-term problem, and sometimes it adjusts future plans to rectify a larger problem in future funding cycles.

The long lead times associated with the funding process—acquisition lead times on the order of six months to several years, planning and programming lead times on the order of two to six years—place a premium on developing an effective, financially achievable, initial plan—before execution begins. During the Cold War era, such plans could be developed over time, because the force structure was relatively stable, as were the changes in the combat support system. Then, it was possible to review current or recent performance, adjust the current plan for some marginal changes, and begin executing the revised plan with high confidence in its cost-effectiveness and feasibility.

However, if the past decade-and-a-half is any indication, it will be more difficult and more risky to use past experience as a resource-allocation planning guide for the foreseeable future. The Air National Guard's force structure has already changed substantially, and more changes are being proposed to roles and missions, force structure, and operational concepts, some of which are detailed in the rest of this monograph. Indeed, the current Quadrennial Defense Review (QDR) seeks to identify new military options for managing previously unanticipated threats, which will inevitably lead to more changes in the ANG.

To participate in such strategy reviews, to help shape their outcomes, and to develop effective implementation plans, the Air National Guard needs a more prospective methodology to evaluate alternative force structures or combat support structure changes before they are implemented or even selected for implementation. Armed with such information, senior leaders can help identify which roles and missions may be best suited for the ANG and the resources needed to achieve the intended level of operational capability. Specifically, they need to be able to test how proposed changes in force structure, funding, or other resources might affect their ability to deliver the required combat capabilities.

Transformational Concept: Developing a Forward-Looking, Combat Support Planning System to Enhance Strategic Planning

As does the rest of the Air Force, the Air National Guard uses its financial resources to develop military capabilities that the nation's leaders can use to protect the national interests. In the past, military analysts often compared counts of aircraft by mission design (for example, fighters, bombers) to determine how much combat capability a particular force may have. In many cases, they used aircraft performance data or actual combat experience to estimate how well particular aircraft or fleets of different aircraft would perform against a potential adversary.

Unfortunately, most of those analyses made assumptions about the combat support system and what it could deliver—assumptions that were rarely tested, except in actual combat. Those analyses rarely, if ever, considered the actual operational suitability, airworthiness, or availability of the aircraft.

By *operational suitability,* we mean the ability of a particular aircraft design, including modifications, to deliver the military capabilities required at a particular point in time. Thus, an aircraft that is operationally suitable for one mission may be unsuitable for another. More important, operational suitability is ephemeral, because advancing adversaries' capabilities may marginalize or even eliminate a fleet's ability to perform its intended mission over time. For example, the development of stealth has marginalized the effects of integrated air defense systems by eliminating the warning and reducing the accuracy of ground-to-air defenses.

By *airworthiness,* we mean the aircraft's inherent flight safety. That, too, is inherently ephemeral. If an aircraft is left unmaintained for a long enough time, material discrepancies will emerge that steadily increase the risks of flying that aircraft. Even maintenance cannot guarantee that an aircraft will last forever; sooner or later, metal fatigue or other material limitations will make it exceedingly expensive to return an aircraft to an airworthy status.

Finally, by *availability,* we mean *net* availability, or the product of the fraction of the whole fleet that is both possessed by the operating commands and in mission capable status. Availability is perhaps the most ephemeral of all these factors. To prevent airworthiness problems resulting from the structure of the aircraft, the Air Force and the Air National Guard periodically remove aircraft from service to conduct field, depot, or contractor inspections intended to ensure that no structural problems exist. To ensure that the aircraft are operationally suitable, field maintenance personnel respond to aircrews' reported operational problems and conduct independent screening processes designed to detect, diagnose, and remedy the effects of failed or marginal operational performance by replacing critical mission related components from limited local stocks. Shops in the field, at depots, and at contractor repair sites repair those components and return them to local stocks.

We do not mean to imply that previous analyses of missions or capabilities ignored issues associated with operational suitability, airworthiness, or availability. Rather, we mean that, although those analyses made assumptions about what levels of those three factors the combat support system could deliver, subsequent combat-support budgetary, material, and operational challenges may render those assumptions inaccurate. As a consequence, there is a need to periodically or continually review the challenges facing the combat support system for aircraft, making appropriate adjustments to balance all four factors: operational suitability, airworthiness, availability, and cost.

The relationships among those four factors are complex, as depicted in Figure 4.1. The solid arrows from one ellipse to another indicate that an increase in the originating factor causes an increase in the terminal factor. A dashed line indicates that an increase in the

Figure 4.1
Many Factors Affect the Four Main Factors

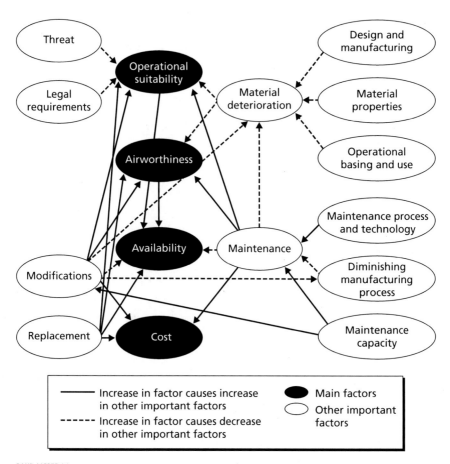

originating factor causes a decrease in the terminal factor. Thus, an increase in the threat or a legal constraint (in the upper-left-hand corner of the figure) causes the operational suitability of the fleet to decline, but an expenditure on modifications or a replacement aircraft (in the lower-left-hand corner) can offset such negative effects.

Of course, modifications also increase cost and decrease availability during the period in which the modifications are being implemented. MAJCOMs and the system program directors (SPDs) generally develop the major modification programs to ensure that only a few aircraft are undergoing modification simultaneously, thereby maintaining adequate levels of training and contingency support.

There is a growing body of knowledge about the relationships among these factors for individual weapon systems and fleets. The Air Force Cost Analysis Agency and others have developed cost estimating relationships (CERs) that relate operational tempo, age, and fleet size to costs. Analysts have begun to use the Air Force Total Operating Cost (AFTOC) system to investigate additional CERs. Models have been developed like the Cost Oriented Resource Estimating (CORE) model and Systematic Approach to Better Long-Range Estimates (SABLE) to translate modest changes in force structure or operational tempo into budget estimates.

The Air Force has used models such as the Logistics Composite Model (LCOM) to estimate operational performance levels (for example, sortie rates) extensively. Those models have been used mainly to evaluate current performance levels and manpower requirements to achieve targets—given current operational tempo, aircraft maintenance task labor requirements, and resource mixes and levels. Only recently have analysts begun to study how maintenance, modification workloads, and material-consumption levels may change over time as aircraft age and maintenance concepts evolve. RAND has found consistent life-cycle patterns across a wide range of Air Force aircraft that characterize how those factors change as fleets age (Pyles, 2003).

A forward-looking, combat support planning system would use those or other models, CERs, life-cycle workload patterns, changing fleet ages, retirement and replacement plans, Air Force Cost Analysis Improvement Group (AFCAIG) cost factors, changing force composition, and planned operational tempo to estimate how those factors would interact to affect future budget requirements.

But, a forward-looking planning system should not focus solely on costs. Rather, it needs to be complemented with estimates of output performance, such as sortie rates, availability levels, or mission capable rates. To that end, operational models (that is, models of flow times, resource constraints, and aircraft condition) could be developed to estimate how operational suitability and airworthiness may change as a function of cumulative flying hours, years spent in corrosive environments, age, or (in the case of emerging operational constraints) calendar dates. The analyst could then set thresholds on such measures, representing acceptable levels of each, and then use the force structure, operating plans, future maintenance and modification workload, and material-consumption forecasts to estimate how much of each fleet might pass its thresholds over time.

For example, the growth of fatigue cracks could be modeled in equivalent damage hours, then the fleet's planned operational tempo and historical sortie profiles could be used to estimate when the current fatigue life limit would be reached—that is, when the fleet's airworthiness might be in jeopardy. An analyst need not stop there but could also assess: alternative plans for introducing a service life extension program (SLEP) that would extend the aircraft's operational service life past its original design life, then evaluate the cost-effectiveness of such an option, compared to replacing the fleet. Of course, that life extension program would require removing some aircraft from service while the modifications were undertaken, reducing the fleet's availability.

Of course, such computations are already done by the SPDs' and original equipment manufacturers' engineers, based on much more detailed studies of the current fatigue and corrosion condition of today's fleets, the anticipated usage of those fleets, and the detailed models of specific critical points in each fleet's design. What we suggest is that options be developed for different levels of funding and that both the funding and the other three factors for each option be presented throughout the planning, programming, and budgeting process so that senior stakeholders and decisionmakers can weigh the maintenance and modification of existing fleets against other funding priorities.

Thus, the most important thing one could do with a forward-looking combat support planning system would be to evaluate trade-offs among the four factors. That is, the ANG could explore alternate solutions in light of the changing threat, the anticipated material deterioration, available maintenance resources, and available funds, if such a system were available.

It is a demanding task to assemble even one fleet's cost information for recent activities. It is even more difficult to estimate how those costs would change for the current year, the year following, and so on, for the Future Years Defense Plan (FYDP)—even if no operational or policy changes occur. Of course, operational and policy changes do occur that affect fleet size; operational tempo; maintenance requirements; modifications planned and under way; and the costs of equipment, spares, personnel, and other resources. Indeed, the process is so complex that DoD has begun to develop its program plans on a biannual, rather than an annual, basis.

Even that process examines alternate cases, but usually those cases are relatively small deviations from a base case. Perhaps more important, there is usually not time to evaluate the operational implications of all those deviations, such as how a reduced modification budget may affect the future airworthiness or operational suitability of an aircraft.

Facing the large changes that may be forthcoming, the Air National Guard needs to be able to examine the implications of many different force structures and combat support options. In addition, it needs to be able to understand how those changes will affect all four factors in Figure 4.1.

It is not possible to construct such a wide-ranging exploration of possible alternatives with the current labor-intensive planning and programming process. Rather, it will be necessary to augment that process with computational procedures that simulate the implementation of alternate resource allocation decisions or policies.

The ANG does not control all the concerns that affect the four factors, but it can influence many of them, as shown in Figure 4.2. Each of the gray ellipses indicates decisions that the Air National Guard either makes or can influence in coordination with the active component of the Air Force.

The Air National Guard does not operate alone in making decisions about how its weapon systems will be acquired, replaced, deployed, operated, modified, maintained, stored, or disposed. Many other agencies influence these factors, including the planners, programmers, and analysts in the active component Major Air Commands, who provide an integrating lead role over the force structure, modification, and sustainment decisions for individual fleets; the system program directors, who are responsible for the technical inte-

Figure 4.2
ANG Influences Some Driving Factors, but Not All

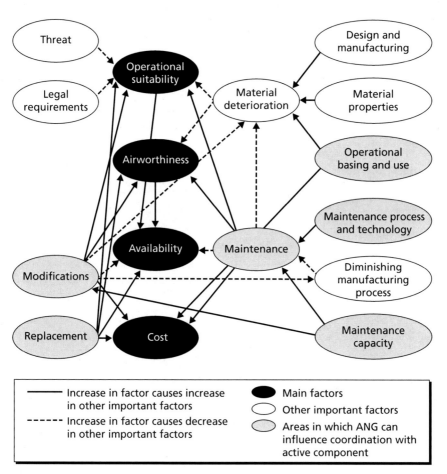

gration of the acquisition, maintenance, modification, and disposal actions regarding a fleet; and the Headquarters Air Force planners, programmers, and budget analysts, who are responsible for ensuring a fiscally balanced and budgetarily sound total program for the Air Force. Officials in all these agencies have something to contribute to the development of an integrated force structure and combat support plan—and a stake in the outcome.

Thus, a forward-looking force structure and combat support planning process must also enable the participation of all the stakeholders, who must be able to contribute their insights, resource requirements, and other constraints to the analyses, and who must also be able to view the results and suggest alternative solutions.

Analytic Approach

RAND developed the Force Structure and Cost Estimating Tool to support its own research on aging Air Force aircraft. However, we believe that it could provide a useful starting point for a forward-looking, combat support planning extension to GUARDIAN. In addition to the issues of funding requirements for a changing fleet composition, it can support making trade-offs across platforms, across missions, or across time. More important, it can also provide a comprehensive view of the relevant conditions of each fleet or mission area.

Specifically, the FSCET is designed to help different agencies cooperatively develop and assess fleets' operational suitability, airworthiness, availability, and operations and maintenance (O&M) costs over time. That is, it is intended to be a corporate tool for which different stakeholders and analytic agencies provide data, suggest alternative support options or concepts, and suggest different force structures and operational tempos that they jointly assess against a background of changing threats and Air Force capability requirements. To that end, it is Web-based so that analysts and stakeholders at different locations can create cases, review results, and suggest improvements without daily face-to-face interaction.

At its core, FSCET provides a simulation of one or more fleets' operation over an extended period. The computational engine within the tool uses a list of initial conditions of the fleet (for example, fleet age profiles, possessing commands, cumulative flying hours), plus analyst-specified plans for future force-structure changes, resource utilization factors, and resource cost factors. The proposed changes to the existing fleet are specified in a group of rules that govern the changes that will occur over the simulation period. Because the rules and initial conditions are specified outside the engine, the analyst may use a variety of different rules that represent different policies or resource-utilization and cost assumptions to examine how the future costs and fleet condition will vary over time.

Thus, FSCET roughly mimics the operation of the fleet operators and supporters, at the individual fleet, MAJCOM, component, or Air Force level. As shown in Figure 4.3, it operates on an annual basis, sequentially adding a year to the existing fleets' ages, applying rules intended to replace or retire individual fleets, computing the condition (material deterioration, modification status, etc., are maintained in nonmonetary accounts), transferring aircraft among commands, estimating budget requirements, allocating the available budgets (rules are available to specify how budget shortages are addressed), then computing new aircraft status and obligations before performing the process all over for the next year.

Analytically, the FSCET computational engine is an expected-value, annualized, time-driven simulation of an entire force composed of many different resources spread across different organizational elements, projecting the effects of changing force structure, posture, technologies, and maintenance efforts on the force's capabilities, availability, and costs over time. It develops a longitudinal data file of the status, costs, and other key attributes of each fleet in each command, for each age group for every year in the simulation. A complementary data analysis tool provides a way to summarize or selectively review how costs or other attributes of individual fleets or groups of fleets vary over time for alternative force structures and

Figure 4.3
FSCET: Simulation Process

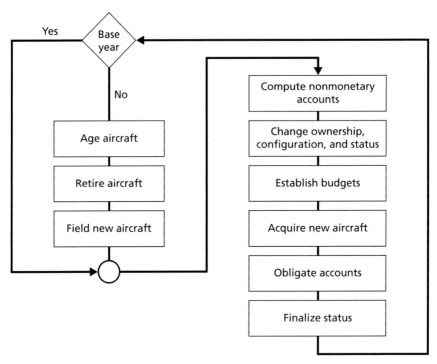

support plans. A case editor, which permits the community of analysts and stakeholders to construct or modify the models, supports those computational and analysis functions.

Individual offices would typically begin their analyses by drawing on an "approved" standard case (ideally, the latest approved plan for allocating resources to different fleets), then would independently examine options and propose promising options to the rest of the community for further evaluation and integration. As specific options are found effective or cost-effective, they can be presented to higher authorities for approval and then used to update the base case for further analyses. In this way, analyses in different offices can be kept synchronized on key decisions while permitting the individual offices wide latitude to evaluate and propose changes to the "currently approved" plan.

To support that community effort, the FSCET case forum also provides a bulletin board for the analysts and stakeholders to discuss each case or a group of cases associated with a project, as depicted in Figure 4.4. Stakeholders can review and comment on shared cases as they are being developed, to correct errors, improve assumptions, and suggest different cases that may be required to analyze a particular option. While formal meetings will still be necessary to make final decisions and to brief senior decisionmakers, the technical analysts can review each other's cases, suggest corrections or improvements, and ensure that the analyses are complete and that all points of view are heard before final decisions are made.

Sometimes, it will not be appropriate to disseminate preliminary results from speculative runs intended to examine sensitive issues or

Figure 4.4
Force Structure and Cost Estimating Tool

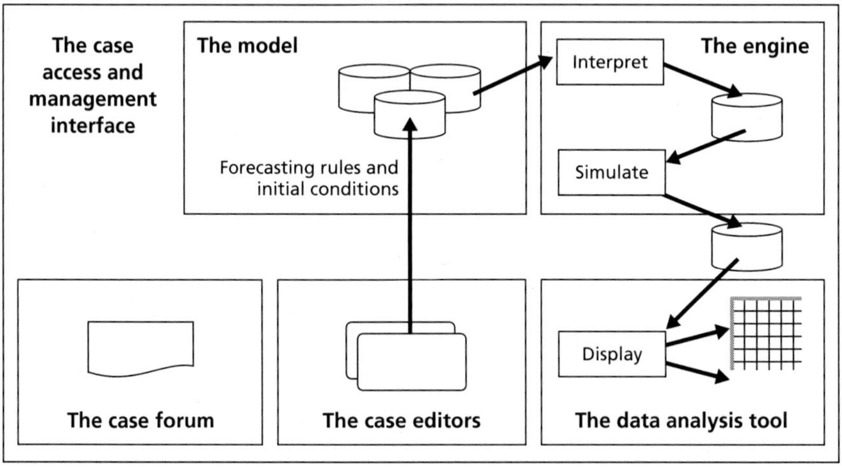

extreme cases. To support such closely held analyses, FSCET also provides a facility for limiting access to sensitive cases or projects, based on which users are authorized to view which projects or cases.

This facility may be useful during the normal planning process, for when one agency or another would like to investigate options privately that might be considered sensitive if erroneous or incomplete information were made widely available prematurely. Thus, multiple agencies could start with a common official base case, then create private cases that evaluate and refine changes to the official plan, and share the results when they had been verified.

Sample Uses of FSCET

So far, most of this chapter has been very abstract, first indicating the kinds of forward-looking assessments of force structure and combat support resource options that the ANG might find valuable, then suggesting that the FSCET may be a prototype for such assessments. We turn now to some examples that demonstrate the kinds of analyses that FSCET can support. We have selected four different examples that may be of interest to the Air National Guard: forecasting KC-135 fleetwide costs, estimating the effects of F-16C/D modifications on that fleet's operational suitability, examining potential risks to future KC-135 airworthiness, and estimating the number of C-5A/B aircraft that will be available, given projected workload growth and current programmed depot maintenance capacity.

Using FSCET to Forecast Maintenance and Modification Costs

The most direct use of FSCET is to estimate future O&M costs. Here, we demonstrate how to use the tool with official data and some CERs to forecast O&M costs.

Figure 4.5 portrays the process diagrammatically. It shows from where we received data for this example and how we used it to estimate how the Air Force's total maintenance costs would vary over the next several decades. The top two rows of shapes address our data

Figure 4.5
FSCET Budgets O&M Costs over Time

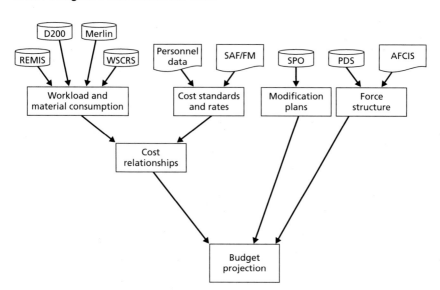

NOTES: SAF/FM = Assistant Secretary of the Air Force, Financial Management and Comptroller; SPO = system program office; WSCRS = Weapon System Cost Recovery System.
RAND *MG375-4.5*

sources and the lower two rows address our processing of those data (by looking at cost relationships and budget projections).

Table 4.1 shows just a few of the official Air Force data tables we incorporated in the tool for our examples.[1] Because the tables are user-modifiable, they can be updated as the factors change, either manually or through the use of comma-separated value (csv) files. By maintaining a standard library of such tables, the analyst can begin individual analyses with little or no work to collect the data.

As shown in Figure 4.5, we used historical maintenance data from standard official sources, including Reliability & Maintainability Information System (REMIS), the D041/D200 DLR require-

---

[1] These tables are available on the Air Force portal.

Table 4.1
Numerous Factor Tables Built into FSCET, but Can Be Updated

Table	Source
Aviation fuel consumption rate	Command Unique Mission Design Series (MDS) AFFUEL Factor Summary, FY2000, AFI 65-503, p. A13-1 (SAF/FMB Web site, January 2005).[a]
Inflation	USAF Raw Inflation Indices, based on OSD Raw Inflation Rates, FY2003, AFI 65-503 (SAF/FMB Web site, January 2005).[a]
Aircraft age–related factors	(Years since acceptance, cumulative flying, corrosion exposure) Program Data System Extract (AF/SPXP, March 2003)
Aircraft configuration	(Flyaway cost, engine weight, engines per aircraft, augmenter, engine fan, engine age (2003), CLS, PDM interval, PDM start). AFI 65-503 (SAF/FMB Web site, January 2005)[a]; U.S. Air Force, *Engine Handbook*, OC-ALC/LP, 2002.
Aircraft operational tempo	(Annual flying hours per PAA, crew ratio, flying hours per crew, annual landings). AFI 65-503, pp. A42-2, A43-1, A44-1 (SAF/FMB Web site, January 2005).[a]
Squadron personnel cost factors	AF 65-503, pp. A42-1, A43-1, A44-1, A19-2, A27-1, A22-1, A23-1 (SAF/FMB Web site, January 2005).[a]
Depot labor rates	Depot Maintenance Activity Group (DMAG) Annual Report (summarized in Air Force Working Capital Fund [AFWCF] Supplement to President's Budget Submission, February 2005).

[a] This Web site is not accessible to the general public.

ments system, and the Air Force Cost Analysis Agency's published tables, directly. In addition, we used data from REMIS and other maintenance sources to develop a set of workload and material-consumption life-cycle relationships.[2] Because the full range of Air Force fleets is used in the historical analysis, we anticipate that those

---

[2] Those equations and the associated analysis are reported in Pyles (2003).

relationships would also generalize to future fleets. Of course, technological improvements or changing operational demands may occur that change those relationships. Therefore, it will be necessary to review those relationships occasionally to ensure that they still apply as the fleets and operating stresses change.

Those relationships differed according to the workload content (for example, base versus depot and on-equipment versus off-equipment) and material-consumption category. We embedded them in our model as equations that could be used to estimate how workloads or material consumption would vary as fleets aged, and how replacing one fleet with another would affect the overall costs.

In addition, we selectively incorporated modernization plans developed by SPDs, for estimating how fleet-modernization costs would change if the fleet structure or the modification schedule were to change.

For the initial force structure, we began with a force structure composed of every Air Force fleet, based on the Air Force Program Data System, or PDS. The PDS is a detailed compilation of the status and condition of each aircraft in the Air Force inventory, including its date of acceptance by the Air Force (from which we derived age), its cumulative flying time, and owning command as of a particular date. While any number of sources may be used to develop alternative force structure modernization plans, we used the Air Force Capabilities Investment Strategy (AFCIS) as a base case against which to compare excursions. Although we have not used the AFCIS extensively, the tool also has the capability to track acquisition expenditures as the force structure is modernized.

Using those data as a starting point, we then used FSCET to develop an Air Force and Air National Guard annual operations and maintenance budget projection for the next several decades. We explore those results in the next section.

The light gray boxes in Figure 4.6 show the actions we took to examine the effects of material deterioration, changing threats, changing legal requirements, and modifications to offset those emerg-

Figure 4.6
FSCET's Expanded Focus—Operational Suitability, Airworthiness,
Availability, Budgets, and Capability over Time

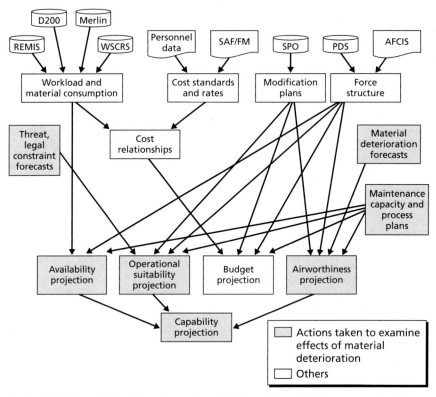

NOTES: SAF/FM = Assistant Secretary of the Air Force, Financial Management and Comptroller; SPO = system program office; WSCRS = Weapon System Cost Recovery System.
RAND MG375-4.6

ing trends. As shown in the figure, we used forecasts of emerging legal requirements for international air channel use, the increasing requirement for improved (net-centric) responsiveness, and a fleet's projected safe operating life limit to examine selected fleets' operational suitability and airworthiness. Then, we examined how selected modifications might change those outcomes. Specifically, we examined the fiscal year 2002 (FY2002) program for introducing net-centric modifications into F-16C aircraft, and we examined how rapidly the KC-135 aircraft fleet might pass the point where the *KC-135 Economic Service Life Study* (Sperry, 2001) hypothesized that fleet might need a replacement of the upper wing skin.

Just as with major programmed depot maintenance (PDM) work, much of the work for such modifications requires temporarily removing aircraft from service. We have developed two prototype co-models (Loredo, Pyles, and Snyder, 2005) to estimate the aircraft available for operations (that is, those not removed from service) that we plan to embed in a future version of FSCET that estimates the number of aircraft undergoing modification and PDM based on considerations of the depot maintenance resources available.

From the three measures of availability, operational suitability, and airworthiness, cross-fleet measures of capability within FSCET can be derived. That is, the number of available, operationally suitable, and airworthy aircraft with a particular operational capability can be aggregated, perhaps even giving different fleets different weights. For example, tankers could be evaluated on the basis of fuel delivered in a particular scenario (or in several different scenarios), or the cargo capacity could be estimated in million-ton-miles of the cargo fleets, or how many net-centric aircraft could be put aloft at a given time could be estimated. Thus, it should be possible to use FSCET to estimate how much combat capability of a particular kind might be available over time, and to estimate what maintenance and modification investments may be necessary to improve those outcomes.

Using FSCET to Estimate Future ANG KC-135 Maintenance Costs

Figure 4.7 portrays the computations regarding one fleet in detail: the Air National Guard on-equipment maintenance labor costs for KC-135 tankers. All of the graphs are directly from the FSCET data analysis tool. When the particular portrayal of a result is deemed satisfactory, the data can be downloaded into a spreadsheet file for a more formal presentation.

Beginning in graph a, we can observe how one recent fleet replacement plan would modify the future tanker force structure.

Figure 4.7
Computing the ANG On-Equipment Workload Costs

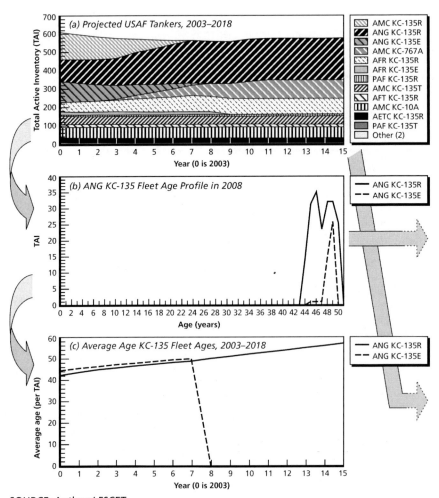

SOURCE: Authors' FSCET.
NOTE: AETC = Air Education and Training Center.
RAND MG375-4.7a

Figure 4.7
Continued

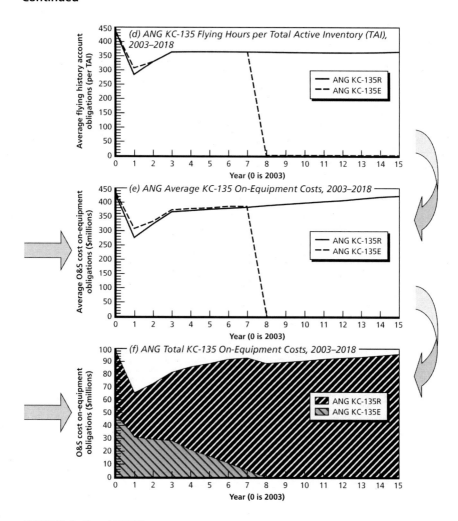

SOURCE: Authors' FSCET.
RAND *MG375-4.7b*

Broadly, this plan called for the KC-135E fleet to be retired early and replaced by a new KC-767A aircraft. As a consequence of that broad plan, the retiring ANG and AFRC KC-135Es would be replaced by KC-135R aircraft transferred from Air Mobility Command (AMC). Thus, the number of KC-135Rs in the ANG and AFRC gradually grows, whereas the KC-135E fleet declines to zero in 2011.

The effect of that on the ANG KC-135 mission design series' (MDS') age profile is shown in graph b. By 2008, almost all of the KC-135Es (dashed curve) are gone, and the ANG force consists mostly of KC-135Rs (solid curve), whose ages range from 44 to 50 years. Graph c shows that the average ages of the KC-135E fleet grow slightly less than one per year, starting in 2005, as the oldest aircraft in the fleet are retired first. (The sudden reduction in 2011 occurs because there are no KC-135Es in the inventory from that date onward.)

Graph d portrays the projected ANG operational flying program that will be required to maintain the projected pilot availability. (Peacetime training requirements depend on the number of crews available per aircraft and the flying required to maintain existing pilots' skills and to upgrade co-pilots' skills to enable them to become pilots. Changing the crew ratio would also change the flying program and the fleets' demands for flying-related maintenance and material.) The initial value (in 2003) is due to the operations associated with supporting Operation Iraqi Freedom (OIF). Over the next three years, the plan called for returning to pre-OIF levels in 2004, but gradually increasing the crew ratio to a new, steady-state level in 2006 and beyond. Thus, the flying hours required of each aircraft will increase, and so will some maintenance costs (demands for maintenance are driven by flying hours).

Graph e shows how the changing KC-135R age profile, the flying program drop in 2004, and the subsequent rise through 2006 would interact to affect future on-equipment maintenance labor costs for each aircraft in ANG's total inventory (that is, including those in depot and modification status). As we can see, the planned temporary flying program dip (in graph d) shows up as a similar dip in the average on-equipment maintenance labor hours required per aircraft in the early years, but the labor requirements continue to grow at a modest rate after the flying program stabilizes, as a result of fleet age on on-equipment maintenance labor requirements.

Graph f combines the age- and operational tempo–based average aircraft effects with the effects of the changing force structure on overall ANG on-equipment labor requirements over time, with the (rising) KC-135R costs in the top pattern; the (diminishing) KC-135E costs (bottom pattern) reflect the replacement of the KC-135E fleet by the KC-135R fleet. Changes in operational tempo dominate the early years' requirements through 2006, the KC-135R requirements gradually replace the KC-135E requirements through 2012, and the aging effect leads to a small, long-term growth afterward. Although this figure isolates this specific fleet's costs from those of all the other fleets in the simulation, it provides a detailed analysis of how the different operations and maintenance cost elements for that fleet may evolve if the projected plan is adopted.

Of course, operations and maintenance costs are not limited to on-equipment labor at the flight line. Figure 4.8 portrays how the ANG KC-135 cost elements we modeled in this example would change in the future, if that plan were implemented.

Graphs a and b portray the KC-135E and KC-135R cost structure over time in some detail; graphs c and d provide a summary overview across the two MDSs. In graphs a and b, we can see the ANG overall costs for the KC-135E diminish, but its total KC-135R costs increase, at first because of the fleet replacement program, then because of age. The top-five costs in both graphs are the war reserve base maintenance (that is, the portion of maintenance time not fully used in peacetime, but required for the much higher wartime operational tempo), the PDM, fuel, on-equipment workloads, and base operating support (BOS).

In graph c, we can see that the overall ANG KC-135 PDM costs are growing noticeably but that the other accounts have only a modest effect on total costs over the projected 15-year period. In graph d, the plan's shift from expenditures for KC-135Es (gray) to KC-135Rs (diagonal pattern) is clear.

Figure 4.8
More Than On-Equipment Direct Labor: ANG KC-135 Operations and Maintenance Costs

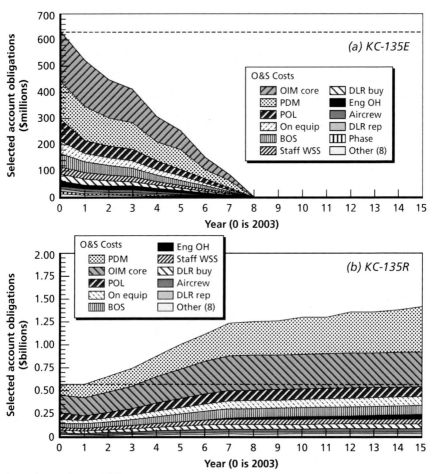

SOURCE: Authors' FSCET.
NOTES: BOS = base operating support; DLR = depot-level repair; EngOH = engine overhaul; OIM = the cost of maintenance labor that is kept available for wartime operations but that is unused (except for training) in peacetime; WSS = weapon system security personnel costs (the additional cost of security personnel to guard the aircraft and the squadron, not those needed to establish basic base security).
RAND *MG375-4.8a*

**Figure 4.8
Continued**

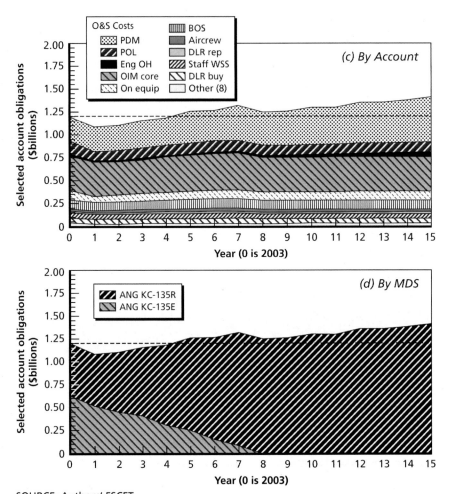

SOURCE: Authors' FSCET.
NOTES: BOS = base operating support; DLR = depot-level repair; EngOH = engine overhaul; OIM = the cost of maintenance labor that is kept available for wartime operations but that is unused (except for training) in peacetime; WSS = weapon system security personnel costs (the additional cost of security personnel to guard the aircraft and the squadron, not those needed to establish basic base security).
RAND *MG375-4.8b*

In passing, we note that the FSCET cost categories we used can be mapped directly to the familiar categories established by the AFCAIG. Most of those mappings are on a one-to-one basis, but our analysis of previous base-level maintenance workload life-cycle patterns found markedly different life-cycle growth patterns for different workloads. Consequently, we disaggregated the AFCAIG base-level aircraft maintenance category into on-equipment, off-equipment, phase/isochronal, and special inspection categories in this FSCET example. (FSCET can accept any workload or cost account categories.) We used the AFCAIG categories for this example, but any other accounting framework can be accommodated. Indeed, we could have aggregated the various base-maintenance workload categories into a single base-maintenance cost category, but then important information about the primary source of cost growth (on-equipment maintenance at the flight line) would have been obscured.

First, note that FSCET displays the various categories according to the size of the change they experience during the interval. Thus, PDM, which undergoes the largest change, is displayed on top, followed by "OIM core," and then by a number of other cost categories with progressively smaller changes.

The ANG KC-135R PDM workload account is projected to grow more than any other as a result of an increasing force structure combined with a growing PDM workload per aircraft. The force-structure changes dominate the first seven years of the growth; the slower growth beginning in 2012 is due to the fleet's aging.

The second-largest change is in "OIM core," OIM core is computed as the base-level maintenance man-hours available in the base year that cannot be explained by the workload computed by the life-cycle maintenance workload equations for that year. It represents the maintenance labor hours available after such things as sick leave and vacation time for this MDS in this command, but not used for peacetime aircraft maintenance. Those unutilized maintenance labor hours represent a spare base-level capacity often used for other military duties in peacetime, and they also represent a war reserve capacity for maintenance demands that may arise in wartime. In our analyses, we held OIM core per total active inventory (TAI) constant over time, allowing base-level maintenance costs to increase only for forecast workload growth. (Another option would be to increase base-level personnel in proportion to the workload, but doing so does not reflect current Air Force or ANG policy or practice.) The growth in expenditures for this account is due solely to the change in the force structure.

In a similar manner, the change in costs in most of the other categories shown (petroleum, oil, and lubricants [POL], on-equipment maintenance, base operating support [BOS], squadron staff and weapon system security, depot-level repair [DLR] buys, aircrews, DLR, and eight other smaller categories) are due mainly to changes in the force structure and operational tempo, although small, age-related growth is present in on-equipment, off-equipment, and DLR maintenance activities.

In contrast, the engine-overhaul workload growth shown is due not to the force-structure change but to the gradual aging of the KC-135R engines. The overhaul costs for that engine are currently quite modest; however, the historical growth patterns in Air Force engine overhauls suggest that those costs will emerge as a noticeable factor early in the next decade of KC-135R operations. Even so, those costs will be dwarfed by the aircraft PDM workload account.

Using FSCET to Estimate Future F-16C/D Fleet Operational Suitability

We now turn to an example of using FSCET to characterize changing operational suitability. For this example, we use the recent F-16 modification program plan outlined in Appendix P3 to the *FY2003 President's Budget* (2003 PB) (The White House, 2002). Both active component and ANG units operate aircraft in this fleet and as we shall see, the plan outlined in Appendix P3 to the 2003 PB may not modify the ANG F-16C/D fleet as rapidly or as completely as the active fleet.

As shown in Figure 4.9, the 2003 PB identified 16 different modification activities under way or proposed for implementation in the F-16C/D fleet, each with a separate funding stream. Each modification is identified in the chart by its Mission Essential Needs

Figure 4.9
F-16C/Ds with Each Modification Complete (Total Force)

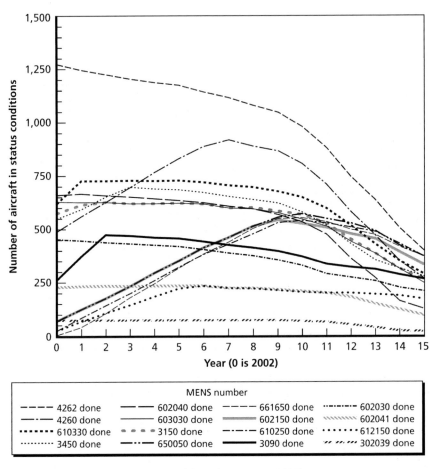

SOURCE: *FY2003 President's Budget* (The White House, 2002).
RAND *MG375-4.9*

Statement (MENS) number. The 2003 PB included modifications that were in various stages of development, some that were planned to be fully implemented by the end of FY2002 and others just beginning installation in 2003. (The 2003 PB was submitted to Congress in 2002, so it included information on tasks to be completed in that year.) Each line in the figure reflects the number of F-16C/D aircraft that would have completed each modification according to the 2003 PB. Thus, the top, downward-sloping curve in the figure reflects a modification that was to be completed in the F-16C/D aircraft in 2002 and the other lines that generally rise, then fall, reflect the installation of other modifications. The downward slope of the top line reflects only the expected aircraft attrition through 2011 (based on the official Air Force attrition equation with F-16 parameters), after which the F-16C/D fleet size declines more rapidly as the planned F-35 acquisition program finishes replacing F-16A/Bs and starts to replace F-16C/Ds.

Of course, one would need to know a great deal about each MENS to understand how all those modifications might contribute to the F-16C/D fleet's operational suitability. We used the matrix depicted in Table 4.2 to help summarize six MENS' effects on F-16C/D net-centric capabilities, which can be related to operational suitability. As one can see from the matrix, the first four MENS establish a basic net-centric operational capability for the F-16C/D by providing the communications and target-designation links to make the aircraft capable of responding quickly to targets located and identified by other participants in the network. The fifth MENS enhances that baseline capability by adding a more direct link to ground observers, further reducing the response time. The sixth MENS adds a nighttime operations dimension to the baseline capability.

Inputting the data from this matrix into FSCET, we were able to construct a more succinct assessment of the joint effects of those

Table 4.2
Net-Centric View of F-16C/D Avionics Modifications

Mission Need	Baseline	Ground Support	Night Operations	Ground and Night
MN602150	X	X	X	X
MN610250	X	X	X	X
MN65005	X	X	X	X
MN661650	X	X	X	X
MN4262		X		X
MN602040			X	X

six MENS, as depicted in Figure 4.10. This figure displays how the current F-16C/D fleet modification plans will gradually increase that fleet's capability to participate in net-centric operations. Using the

Figure 4.10
Operational-Suitability Forecast—Air Force and ANG F-16C/D Net-Centric Capability

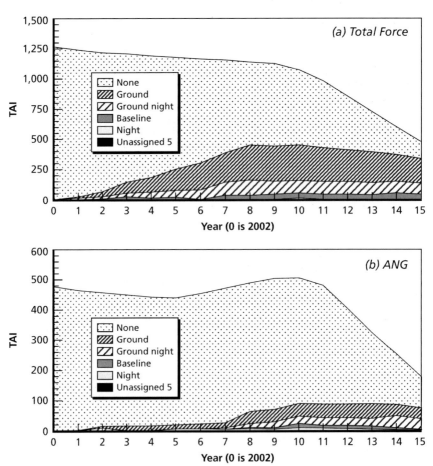

SOURCE: Author's FSCET.

RAND *MG375-4.10*

MENS-to-capability translation matrix in Figure 4.9, we were able to integrate the contributions of those modifications to the fleet's net-centric capability.

A key assumption in our analysis was that the Air Force would choose to make the 16 modifications to those aircraft with the larger remaining operational service lives. Thus, our FSCET modification rule specified that the modification would be installed on the youngest aircraft in the fleet.

The topmost area in graph a indicates the number of F-16 aircraft in the Total Air Force that have no net-centric capability, over time; the next area shows those with ground support capability; and the area under that has both ground support and night enhancements. In essence, this plan would ultimately convert almost half of the total F-16C/D fleet and provide almost all converted aircraft with enhanced daytime joint ground capability simultaneously with the baseline capability. It would convert only about 10 percent of the fleet to have both day and night net-centric capability.

Whereas graph a shows that nearly half the total Air Force F-16C/D fleet would have at least ground net-centric capability by 2012, graph b shows that a smaller fraction of the ANG F-16C/D fleet would be modified under the plan. This disparity occurred because the ANG has most of the older aircraft that would not receive modifications under our rule, and the then-current (2003) Air Force Capabilities Investment Strategy (AFCIS, an 18-year fleet replacement plan) did not reflect any specific plan to transfer the newer (modified) F-16C/Ds to the ANG as the F-35 is fielded.

Using FSCET to Assess KC-135 Airworthiness

We turn now to assessing airworthiness with FSCET, using the KC-135 fleet as an example. While much of the FSCET's modeling focus has been on the issue of changing budget requirements over time as force structure and fleet ages change, the tool also has the ability to compute and track other attributes of the represented fleets. Although the tool does not (usually) project and track the information about individual aircraft, it does project and track those attributes for aircraft within the same age cohort, by MDS and operating command. That is, it can keep track separately of the average flying hours or other attributes for aircraft that are currently 45 years old and of aircraft that are 46 years old, etc.

In this example, we initialized the ages of the KC-135 fleet age cohorts in 2003 with the average cumulative flying hours reported in the Air Force PDS data system as of December 31, 2003. Then, using the various MAJCOM's programmed flying hours, we used the FSCET's capabilities to update and track those values over time.

We then turned to engineering experts' judgment about when structural-fatigue problems might emerge for this fleet. In this case, we were able to draw on the *KC-135 Economic Service Life Study* (Sperry, 2001), conducted by an Air Force integrated product team, led by Boeing, whose engineers identified two specific structural modifications that might be required if that fleet were operated until 2040. The first of these modifications was an upper-wing skin re-placement, projected to begin in 2012. (The other modification was to the lower fuselage skins.)

A review of the accumulated flying-hour program indicated that the most heavily flown Air Force age cohorts would pass about 22,000 flying hours in 2012. We adopted that threshold as an ap-proximate level past which aircraft in the fleet might operate at in-creased risk of in-flight structural failures.

Using the FSCET data analysis tool, we asked for a display of how many aircraft from each command would pass that threshold each year if no modification were undertaken. The result is displayed in Figure 4.11. Note that the graph starts in 2003, so year 9 is really 2012. As we can see from the figure, as many as 40 heavily tasked KC-135Rs in AMC would be the first aircraft to pass the threshold about 2011–2013. In the next few years, a few AFRES KC-135E air-craft are projected to pass the threshold in 2017, but the number of aircraft passing the threshold increases sharply in 2018 and beyond. Even then, the risk to the fleet would emerge slowly over the ensuing decade, with the ANG KC-135E/Rs being the last fleets to be af-fected, starting in 2037.

Figure 4.11
KC-135 Fleet Potential Future Risk (Upper-Wing Skin,
Aircraft Flying Hours >22,000)

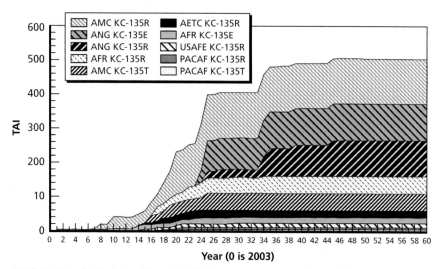

SOURCE: Threshold derived from *KC-135 Economic Service Life Study* (Sperry, 2001),
which identified possible upper-wing skin-replacement requirement circa 2012.
NOTES: AETC = Air Education and Training Center; USAFE = U.S. Air Forces, Europe.
RAND *MG375-4.11*

The *KC-A3: Economic Service Life Study* suggested that a ten-year modification program might be required, commencing in 2012. Such a program would complete the modification well before the 22,000-flying-hour threshold, except for a few of the most heavily flown AMC KC-135Rs.

Using FSCET to Estimate C-5 Availability

In Figure 4.12, we present an example of an analysis for the Air Force Fleet Viability Board (AF FVB). This analysis was performed using a co-model of FSCET (the PDMCAT, or Programmed Depot Maintenance Capacity Assessment Tool), one that we plan to embed in the FSCET as time permits.

As we can see from the figure, recent events have created considerable turbulence in the number of C-5s in PDM status. Those events include the transfer of the workload from the San Antonio Air

Logistics Center (SA-ALC) to the Warner-Robins ALC (WR-ALC), the shift of the C-5B to a seven-year interval between PDMs, and some delayed PDMs in 2002–2003. If the WR-ALC PDM facility were to induct all the aircraft coming due in 2005, it would induce another peak that year, and the number of C-5B aircraft produced would cause another peak about 2012, because they would all need PDM at about the same time.

Of course, the predominant feature of the illustration is what would happen in the middle of the next decade as a result of both the C-5A and C-5B workloads continuing to grow, based on the RAND Project AIR FORCE workload forecasts.[3]

Fortunately, the WR-ALC PDM facility, through a combination of increased capacity and improved process flows, has been able to reduce its flow times substantially over the past few years. For it to continue those improvements would substantially delay the effect of the growing workload on the number of aircraft in PDM status.

Figure 4.12
Sample Availability Forecast: C-5 Aircraft in PDM (SPD Burn Rate)

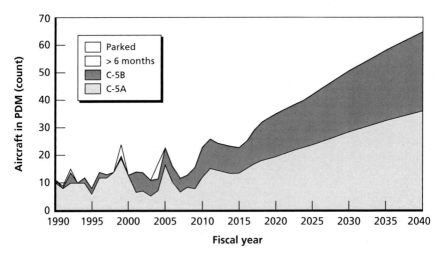

---

[3] See Pyles (2003) for a description of the equation used to forecast PDM workloads.

Air Force and ANG GUARDIAN Implications

The FSCET was designed with the Total Air Force in mind, but it provides an initial capability to examine ANG fleets' airworthiness, operational suitability, availability, and O&S costs. Because the tool is script-driven and because fleets can be defined as needed by the using organization (for example, to the base level), the current FSCET data set and rules to examine ANG-unique issues can be reconfigured. Many of the airworthiness and operational suitability issues associated with aging fleets are likely to fall more heavily on the ANG fleets, along with the consequences of reduced availability and increased O&S costs.

At a minimum, the tool would also help the command estimate the consequences of the coming changes in force structure and operational tempo, thereby supporting the development of the command's inputs to the POM and the longer-range AFCIS.

CHAPTER FIVE

Reachback Options: Costs, Benefits, and Risks

Reachback, whereby warfighters are located away from the area of operations, can be used to reduce the forward-deployed footprint—a desired AEF operational effect. This aspect of the research creates an analytic structure that can be used to determine potential reachback candidates within the current operational environment. In considering potential reachback candidate tasks, we initially evaluated several system or work-process attributes. We considered whether a system or work process was well defined, whether tasks were accomplished primarily using information technology (IT) systems, and whether a mission area had some history of ANG participation. In discussions with Air Force and ANG personnel, the research team quickly identified the Air and Space Operations Center (AOC) as a candidate test environment. Focusing on the Falconer AOC,[1] we found several areas that the team could study and use to clarify the desired characteristics of a reachback candidate. In this chapter, two examples are examined—the air mobility division and the combat operations division—both within the AOC. Each example illustrates a range of options that the Air Force and Air National Guard could choose to implement. These examples are not exclusive (there are many other reachback opportunities), but they are inclusive. The primary focus of this phase of the research is to understand reachback as a potential

---

[1] There are two basic types of AOCs—functional AOCs, such as the mobility air forces' (MAF's) Tanker Airlift Control Center (TACC), and Falconer AOCs, used in the combat air forces (CAF). The Falconer AOC was the focus of the initial research effort, but some basic findings apply to both types.

mission area for the ANG and to create an analytic structure that can be used to select reachback candidates for any command, active duty, Reserve, or National Guard for further study. The chapter begins by discussing the current and transformational concepts associated with reachback.

Current Falconer AOC Practice

A Falconer AOC provides operational-level command and control for the combat air forces (CAF). Its overall focus is on producing and executing the air tasking order (ATO). A typical Falconer AOC comprises five divisions: strategy; combat plans; combat operations; intelligence, surveillance, reconnaissance; and air mobility. The current Warfighting Headquarters plan calls for five Falconer AOCs: one in the Pacific, one in Europe, one in the Central Command area of responsibility, one in Korea, and one in the Southern Command area of responsibility.[2]

Currently, two of the three ANG units (and one Reserve unit) are aligned with a specific Commander, Air Force forces (COMAFFOR) and associated joint forces air component commander (JFACC), if designated by the combatant commander, for AOC augmentation.[3] For example, the 152 NY-ANG in Syracuse, New York, is aligned with the 32 Air Operations Group (AOG) in Ramstein Air Base, Germany, and the 157 MO-ANG in St. Louis, Missouri, is aligned with the 502 AOG in Hickam AFB, Hawaii. During exercises or military operations, personnel from the 152 traveled forward to Germany to augment the AOC on Ramstein. Each Air National Guard unit has a 125-person unit type code (UTC), 7FVX5, which spreads manpower into slots throughout the AOC during augmentation. The practice being used today has all products and tasks completed forward. The ANG does not own a specific task

---

[2] Maj Willard Clark, "WFHQs Briefing—Directors Update," briefing, April 28, 2005.

[3] The State College, Penn., unit is not assigned to a specific area of responsibility (AOR) or COMAFFOR.

or product, but it contributes to the overall manpower to run the AOC.

The ANG approach to augmentation is unit-based. It is not an individual mobilization augmentee (IMA) or individual-based approach as found for some Air Force Reserve Command personnel. The ANG unit maintains administrative and training authority for the augmentation mission. ANG AOG commanders work with the active AOG commander to ensure that personnel meet the warfighter needs. There is a training requirement for local unit infrastructure that the unit maintains and uses to meet qualification and currency requirements. The augmentation model has AOC UTCs training in the local area and deploying forward to the warfighting AOCs they augment.

The Air Force has been struggling with defining how big an AOC needs to be. RAND teams visited the combined AOC (CAOC) in Al Udeid, Qatar. Many of the tasks observed in the CAOC did not require forces to be located forward in the CAOC. Those tasks could have been performed anywhere, including in the continental United States (CONUS). RAND researchers also visited Air Combat Command (ACC) CONUS-based active component intelligence units working with unmanned aerial vehicle Predator data for CAOC commanders located in the Iraqi joint operations area (JOA) during Operation Iraq Freedom (April 2003). RAND teams also observed exercises Terminal Fury 2004, in the Pacific, and Austere Challenge 2004, in Europe. Both exercises employed a Falconer AOC similar to the CAOC in Al Udeid. Again, many tasks were observed that could be moved to the rear. What was needed was an analytic framework, which would help sort tasks and make visible key issues that need further work.

The task of identifying reachback candidates is not an attempt to take apart or reduce a Falconer AOC. The research assumes that what is in a Falconer (for example, IT systems, people, and work processes) is needed by the COMAFFOR and/or JFACC to accomplish their mission. It does ask whether there are tasks that can be completed away from the main AOC site, and, if so, whether some work on these tasks could be done from CONUS. From our observations at Al Udeid and during the Pacific Air Force (PACAF) and U.S. Air Forces, Europe (USAFE) exercises, it appears that reachback to CONUS should be possible. This research attempts to identify which tasks are well suited to being accomplished from CONUS, full- or part-time, by personnel assigned to ANG units with a reachback mission. ANG personnel are successfully meeting augmentation mission requirements. This research investigates what changes with a reachback mission and what is the potential effect on mission success.

Current Air Mobility Division Practice

The Air Mobility Division (AMD) is a division within the Falconer AOC structure. When RAND teams were present during Terminal Fury 2004, we observed that the AMD serving the PACAF staff and reporting to the PACAF/DO was operated by a private company under a contract administered by PACAF. Although directed by an Air Force officer, the AMD in this example had been packaged as a set of tasks and contracted out. We did observe Air Force mobility personnel in the other PACAF AOC divisions. The contract AMD in fact did not sit with the PACAF AOC, but was located in the headquarters building across the street from the hangar that housed the core AOC functions.

The Air Mobility Command has also been evaluating the AMD. AMC has a requirement to make all their AMDs supporting the Falconer AOCs fully operational by 2006. To do so, AMC must increase its currently AMD-tagged manning by approximately 400 personnel. AMC is looking to the ANG to help fulfill this manpower requirement. AMC has written a concept of operations (CONOPS) for augmentation in the AOC-AMDs it supports, similar to the augmentation structure that already exists to fully man the AOC itself. AMC has identified a 50-person UTC that would deploy forward to supply personnel to the AMD during operations. Units in both New York and Missouri are interested in the AMD augmentation mission, but they do not have the manpower authorizations available within their states to accept the mission.

Since the AMD function is contracted out in PACAF and AMC is looking for ANG assistance, we felt this function would be a good candidate for reachback. However, a more formal analytic process was needed to determine whether reachback is feasible.

Current Combat Operations Division Practice

The Combat Operations Division (COD), part of the AOC, is focused on ATO production and replanning. The COD has an Offensive Operations subteam and a Defensive Operations subteam. The COD is manned 24 hours a day, seven days a week in a multi-disciplined team organized around the dynamic targeting/time-sensitive target (DT/TST) kill chain (find, fix/track, target/engage, assess).[4] Most of the activity takes place on the Offensive Operations floor, with personnel in close proximity to one another. We noted from our visits to AOCs during OIF and the two exercises that these key personnel on the floor were backed up by technicians and officers located nearby but in another room, either for floorspace or security reasons. Depending on the workload (number of DT/TST targets or number of forces engaged in DT/TST activity), these personnel reach back into the Intelligence Surveillance Reconnaissance Division (ISRD) and other COD teams (both also located in the AOC) for technical or subject-matter support.

Since personnel off the Offensive Operations floor supported COD functions, we felt this function might be a good candidate for reachback. Again, a more formal analytic process was needed to determine whether reachback is feasible.

---

[4] With the move toward a full-time warfighter headquarters, some Falconer AOCs are moving to a 24-hour COD operation and will monitor peacetime training and support missions, in addition to any operational missions executed for the combatant commander.

Transformational Concept

The current AOC augmentation mission keeps personnel trained and ready to deploy forward to augment the AOC. ANG units train but do not *do* work tasks in garrison. The transformational concept we investigate in this section takes augmentation one step further—process ownership, completing work tasks in garrison. We propose breaking AOC tasks into individual subtasks focusing on a specific product and evaluating whether those tasks could be completed in CONUS. By focusing on a task or product instead of manpower positions, a unit could work together on one task, perhaps even from its home base.

We further propose establishing reachback to infrastructure/ personnel for products and services that AOCs could subscribe to. For example, one unit may be the expert on weapons of mass destruction (WMD). When a unified command has a WMD analysis issue, it could turn to that unit for support and analyses. Again, we need to determine what products and services could be developed in CONUS.

Once potential reachback candidate tasks are identified, several organizational options should be considered—one reachback site for all JFACCs, individual reachback sites for each JFACC (similar to the augmentation arrangement currently being used), or separate geographic locations for different processes, where each location is the expert in a different field. Each of these options would allow for the ANG to grow training or standboard[5] functions involving the ANG in more pieces of the command and control enterprise.

---

[5] A *standboard* consists of the local experts in a field, whether in flying or in developing an ATO.

Analytic Approach

Figure 5.1 illustrates the methodology we developed for evaluating reachback options. We started with the AOC, because we were already familiar with some of the processes included in the AOC and the ANG had a history of AOC support and augmentation. We identified individual products and services and then broke them out into subtasks and functions that produce a specific product. We developed a tool—a decision tree—to apply criteria to determine whether a task can be completed in the rear (diagrammed in the Appendix). The decision tree—a series of questions to which the answer is yes or no—was developed to help nominate potential reachback candidates and can be applied to any task. The answer to a question routes the user down the tree until reaching the end of a branch. The end of the branch will either offer the task as a potential candidate or eliminate the task for reachback.

The methodology produces not one solution but a portfolio of solutions, or options, to choose from. Once we decided that a task could be completed in the rear, we evaluated the different reachback options—all at one location, separate locations, distributed processes. Then, we looked at costs, benefits, and risks associated with each reachback option. In evaluating the costs/benefits/risks, manpower (including active, Reserve, ANG, and blends), infrastructure, U.S. Title 32 or Title 10 authorities,[6] and forward footprint were considered. The end product is a range of possible options for the ANG.

In applying the methodology, we chose two examples to evaluate, both in the Falconer AOC, to help us understand the range of issues affecting the task and the potential to do the task from within CONUS. The first example is in the AMD. The second example is in the Combat Operations Division. Our goal at this point is to better understand the theory and potential consequences of reachback. The tool is also useful in making assumptions about a task or the purpose of a task more visible to the research team.

---

[6] Title 10 authorities are federal authorities. Title 32 authorities are state authorities.

Figure 5.1
Analytic Approach for Evaluating Reachback Options

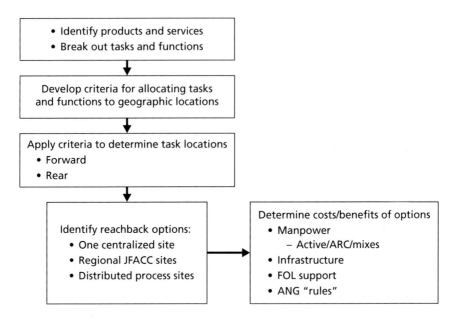

RAND *MG375-5.1*

There are many other potential tasks that could be accomplished with reachback. These are just two illustrative examples that allow us to discuss a wider range of issues.

Preliminary Analysis of the Air Mobility Division

The first example is the Air Mobility Division within the AOC. Although there are mobility personnel in other divisions of the AOC, the AMD is the center for mobility personnel with a background in airlift and aerial refueling tankers in the AOC. The AMD provides products and services to the AOC, which allows the AOC to produce its final product, the air tasking order (ATO). The AMD works with the director of mobility forces (DIRMOBFOR), who works directly for the COMAFFOR/JFACC. The DIRMOBFOR is responsible for the integration of the total air mobility effort for the COMAFFOR/JFACC. The Chief of the AMD ensures that the AMD works as an effective AOC division in the air and space planning and execution process. The AMD coordinates with the parent joint force commander (JFC) movement requirement and control authority, such as the Joint Movement Center (JMC), the theater Air Mobility Operations Control Center (AMOCC) (as appropriate), and the AMC TACC functional AOC at Scott AFB, Illinois (U.S. Air Force, 2002c, Vol. 3, p. 198).

Within the AMD, there are four main missions: to plan, coordinate, task, and execute the air mobility mission. In this example, we look specifically at air mobility planning and execution.[7] We broke those tasks into three subtasks: receives validated requirements (refueling, passenger, cargo, and patient movement), assigns air mobility assets to meet the requirement, and provides air mobility expertise to other AOC division and support services. We ran all three tasks through the decision tree.

Each question in the decision tree calls for a yes or no answer. Depending on how the question is answered, the user will be routed to another question, ending in a final decision of candidate for reachback or not. The decision tree itself is a Microsoft Access database that tracks a user's answers.

It is important to note that assumptions can make a difference in the outcome of the decision tree. Therefore, two people evaluating the same task may come up with a different decision. By tracking each user's answers, we can go back to where different answers were given and discuss the difference. This decision tree was developed to give structure and validity to the reachback issue. There is no one right answer. The decision tree is a means for having a structured dialog about a task and to record the pertinent assumptions and decisions within the discussion. It is a fairly coarse filter, but it does allow the research to be focused better on potential tasks.

---

[7] Although we did not evaluate air mobility coordinating and tasking, they may be good potential reachback candidates.

When we ran the air mobility planning and execution tasks through the decision tree, we made some assumptions that affected the outcome (see the Appendix). For example, when asked, "Does the product require feedback?" we answered yes. The yes answer led us to the next question, "Can the feedback be accomplished by VTC/IWS/telecon [videoteleconferencing/information work space/teleconferencing]?" Again, we answered yes, which led us to the conclusion that the task could be performed through reachback. Several years ago, the answer to "Can the feedback be accomplished by VTC/IWS/telecon" might have been no. Today, with a distributed communications network (for example, chat rooms and other collaborative capabilities) and the appropriate information technology (IT) software/hardware, we assumed the answer to be yes.

We also assumed that the data needed for air mobility planning and execution would be available electronically outside the forward location and that some product-producing capability would still be available in the forward location for unplanned situations.

Again, in working with the tool (decision tree), it is important to note that when a task is being considered for reachback, we are not considering establishing another AOC. We envision removing a specific task from the forward AOC and locating just certain elements of that task in the rear. The reachback site would be part of the existing AOC located forward. Only those tasks that can be completed without face-to-face interaction with the COMAFFOR/JFACC would be considered for reachback. Guidance and direction would still come from the AOC Director, senior division chiefs, and the JFACC and combatant command forward.

After running the three tasks through the decision tree with our assumptions, we identified the first two tasks as potential candidates for reachback—receives validated requirements and assigns air mobility assets to meet the requirement. The third task—provides air mobility expertise to other AOC division and support services—was not identified as a potential candidate. Too much of the third task requires face-to-face interaction with other personnel in the AOC to be performed via reachback.

The three tasks evaluated are performed within five teams in the AMD: the Air Mobility Control Team, the Air Refueling Control Team, the Airlift Control Team, the Aeromedical Evacuation Control Team, and the Air Mobility Element. The question we then posed was, "Where would ANG ownership of the task improve the process?" This question assumes that the ANG could take ownership of a specific task and complete the task from CONUS. In working through the tool, we believe that, depending on the task, there may be more than one "business plan" or CONOPS for how tasks can be completed by a unit using reachback. For example, the ANG could provide a service in CONUS the AOC could subscribe to. That is, the ANG could produce a product that more than one potential user could use. Or, perhaps the ANG could provide specialized infrastructure the warfighter could access. These tasks may include tasks that require a specialized computing capability or deep knowledge or analytic capability. There appear to be many ways in which the ANG could contribute to the air mobility planning and execution mission.

Preliminary Analysis of the Combat Operations Division

The most time-critical function of the AOC is the execution of the ATO and combat operations. To fully understand the challenges presented by reaching back to a remote site for completion of a critical task, we looked for a task requiring timely interface with senior leaders and collaboration with multiple teams within the AOC. This second example evaluates time-critical tasks in the Combat Operations Division of the AOC. We began with the Falconer AOC Flight Manual (U.S. Air Force, 2002c) and looked at AOC critical employment tasks/functions. We chose to evaluate Operations Execution, which is conducted in the Combat Operations Division of the AOC.

The COD is manned 24 hours a day, seven days a week by a multidisciplinary team organized around the dynamic targeting/time-sensitive target (DT/TST) kill chain (find, fix/track, target/engage, assess).[8] The goal of the DT/TST kill chain is to provide the command authority with a shoot decision. DT/TST is very dependent on the situation, available resources, the theater, and/or specific AOC commander procedures. A successful DT/TST starts with good intelligence, a strategy for prosecuting DTs/TSTs to gain a specific desired effect, planning that postures sufficient intelligence, surveillance, and reconnaissance (ISR) and striker forces, and timely command and control (C2) procedures, some of which requires deep knowledge about the target sets, tactical and strategic battlespace, specific platform capabilities, and adversary's tactics and intent. It also requires strict attention to detail and analytic capability that can react to a dynamic tactical environment. That being said, much effort has been spent in providing tools, knowledge, and expertise aimed at executing the operations process. As AOC tools and automation of the ATO process have progressed: Both the number of personnel and the forward footprint have been reduced.

There could be many DT/TST teams within the COD, and the DT/TST teams could be located in separate locations. For example, in one AOC there may be one DT/TST team for operations in Afghanistan and another DT/TST team for operations in Iraq. Or, the DT/TST teams could be located in separate locations, such as during Operation Enduring Freedom: One DT/TST team was at Prince Sultan Air Base, Saudi Arabia, and another was in CONUS. Today, in Operation Iraqi Freedom, much of the ISR sensor exploitation is being accomplished by forces deployed in-garrison who work in a distributed communications network with the forward-deployed AOC. However, the key spot in the AOC for accomplishing the DT/TST work is the COD dynamic targeting officer (DTO), who is one of the Offensive Operations Team officers. As the need develops in a crisis, the DTO calls on a Dynamic Targeting Cell to extend and deepen his/her analytic capability and situational awareness, as well as to increase the ability of the AOC to prosecute multiple targets. The

---

[8] With the move toward a full-time warfighter headquarters, some Falconer AOC are transitioning to a 24-hour COD operation and will monitor peacetime training and support missions, in addition to any operational missions executed for the combatant commander.

increased capability is necessary to achieve the timeliness and precision (and to also avoid collateral damage) desired by the command authority. Since these DT/TST teams have already been used in a reachback mode during Operations Enduring Freedom and Iraqi Freedom, we considered them a good candidate for future reachback options. In all cases we reviewed, however, the DTO was collocated with the commander making the DT/TST decision to shoot, usually in the line of sight of the commander. This was not the case for all the personnel engaged in the complex DT/TST task.

Again, we are not considering establishing another AOC in CONUS. We envision removing specific COD tasks from the forward AOC and locating just the elements of those tasks in the rear. The reachback site would still be part of the existing AOC located forward, with guidance and direction coming from the JFACC and combatant command forward.

The same process used to evaluate the AMD was used to evaluate the COD. We first break the COD down into individual tasks that provide specific products. In this illustration, we concentrated on the DT/TST Combat Operations Team and DT/TST analysis. There are four main tasks performed by the DT/TST Combat Operations Team: find the target, fix/track the target, target/engage the target, and assess the operation. We ran all four tasks through the decision tree.

When we ran COD tasks through the decision tree, we made some assumptions that affected potential outcomes. For example, the very first question asks, "Does the task generate a product?" We answered yes, assuming that in the COD the *product* would be a recommendation to the commander about the target. Another assumption made in this example was that some on-site DT/TST targeting capability would remain forward in the AOC, so that targeting could be done on short notice to satisfy an immediate need. (Feedback may be the important consideration here, with some sensitive targets requiring a commander's action.)

After running the main tasks performed by the DT/TST Combat Operations Team through the decision tree—find the target, fix/track the target, target/engage the target, and assess the operation—with our assumptions, all four tasks were identified as potential candidates for reachback.

We again posed the question, "Could transferring responsibility to the ANG improve the process? In taking ownership of a task, could the ANG be in a better position to provide a more complete answer or product? What strengths would help enable the accomplishment of the task?"

After working though this initial set of tasks, we concluded that there appear to be many ways in which the ANG could contribute to the DT/TST tasks. The full DT/TST process needs several categories of personnel to work tasks necessary to gain sufficient intelligence, planning, and execution capability. In working the DT/TST reachback capability, we have centered the effort on the execution capability located within the COD. If a reachback capability for DT/TST were created within the ANG, certainly some of these other tasks could be bundled into the overall DT/TST force being presented. In fact, some of the strategy and plans tasks are less time-sensitive and are likely candidates for the reachback mission. Certainly the execution function is the most challenging because of the advantage of intrasite communications over remote communications. However, with a limited number of CAF Falconer AOCs, it is doubtful that each JTF and JFACC would have access to a full AOC on-site in the JOA forward area.

Certainly there are other reachback tasks the ANG could immediately engage in as an augmentation unit. Any number of Combat Plans Division tasks—such as operations planning two or more ATO cycles beyond the current cycle—would not have the strict timelines and complicated communications networks needed for successful completion as the DT/TST task does. However, DT/TST supporting tasks are being done in the rear area today. Being able to reach back to a force deployed in-garrison widens the number and expertise of personnel who can be engaged to prosecute a DT/TST target.

This example helped the research team to better understand the question of AOC product, commander oversight (as that of a process) versus insight (as that into a process), and the role and function of feedback in a timely command decision. By observing the DT/TST process in an AOC, we noted that only a portion of the DT/TST team is actually face-to-face on the operations floor. Many people process the information. Each person observes the same data but adds value as their perspective or view allows.

The present augmentation model could be used as a baseline, with the present training infrastructure being used for federal mission work. The reachback option utilizes many of the recognized ANG strengths: First, it would be necessary to determine how best to transition into federal status (Title 10 status) when certain agreed-upon operations thresholds are reached. Second, there would have to be a means for AOC commanders to manage reachback tasking. Finally, a certain amount of investment would be necessary to ensure that reachback units have secure, redundant access to the distributed communications network. There would also have to be investment in mission infrastructure, systems, and software used by the AOC to support the agreed-upon reachback tasks.

We next look at some of the costs and benefits that surfaced in this initial look at reachback missions.

Cost/Benefit Analysis of Reachback Options

Now that we have some potential reachback candidates, we need to evaluate the best method for that reachback. We will investigate three different possibilities: centralized reachback to one location for all COMAFFOR/JFACCs, geographically distributed reachback for each COMAFFOR/JFACC, or functionally distributed reachback for which each geographic location would be the Center of Excellence for a specific function. Each option has different costs, benefits, and risks associated with it. Note that, in the process of working through the analysis, other options may become visible.

Let us take the next step and look at different means for basing reachback missions. In the ANG force presentation, it is important that we acknowledge the significance of each state's individual perspective and create options that are appropriate for the ANG.[9]

One Reachback Location

One method of reachback would be to have only one, centralized, location for all JFACCs to reach back to, with separate cells for each JFACC. For example, Langley Air Force Base could serve as the centralized reachback location. At Langley, there would be a cell dedicated to Central Command, a cell dedicated to Pacific Command, etc. One of the benefits of this option would be the consolidated overhead costs. Only one computer help desk and one administrative staff would be needed. One of the risks would be that all capability would be in one location—making an excellent target for terrorists or another adversary.

This option may require some changes to how UTCs and units are manned to allow for cross-border participation from several states—not just the state where the reachback infrastructure is located. It is not clear that ANG command administrative costs would be less expensive with this option. Each state would still need to retain a Title 32 (state status) cadre to ensure that members are properly accounted for and led. (It is assumed that the member's federal duty location may be in another state, whereas the member's training and administrative functions remain with his/her state ANG.) One way of dealing with staffing to capture savings would be to assign the mission to one state and base members within this same state. However, doing so may isolate the mission and create institutional constraints on accessions and promotions. (A large majority of the work in the AOC requires experienced rated and intelligence personnel who are relatively senior.)

---

[9] Note that it is not our intent to ignore options that would rely on what have been referred to as blended or associate unit presentation. Nor do we want to indicate that cross-border units or UTCs are not possible. This statement notes only that ANG presentation is a state issue as well as a federal issue. The reachback mission needs to be worked within this context.

Many Reachback Locations

A second option is to present forces at geographically separated reachback locations—one per COMAFFOR/JFACC or combatant command JFC.[10] This option is similar to the AOC augmentation arrangement already being used. Currently, each AOC augmentation unit is dedicated to a specific COMAFFOR/JFACC and their parent combatant joint unified command. Adding a reachback capability, each location would continue to be aligned with a COMAFFOR/ JFACC to do appropriate reachback tasks. This option would give the combatant commander oversight over their own reachback location and the personnel engaged in operational command and control tasks. This option also acknowledges the importance of a partnership with an in-theater AOG and its AOC.[11] Each organization can develop deep expertise and knowledge of the operational environment, allies, and potential adversaries in this approach. The approach stresses the ANG strengths of continuity and deep experience by establishing a location at which problems of the area of responsibility (AOR) can be researched in-depth, providing more value than an individual-based augmentation or a more generic facility serving all Falconer AOCs.

One of the costs associated with this option is the potential redundancy in support services. For example, each location would have a computer help desk and administrative services. There would be less flexibility in meeting surge manpower requirements because personnel would be located in many different reachback locations. However, this option eliminates the force-protection risk associated with the

---

[10] This option is similar to the way forces are presented and assigned to the National Security Agency (NSA). The NSA created three major centers at which reachback work is performed for the combatant commanders.

[11] Falconer AOCs are being fielded as a below-the-line warfighter headquarters function, organized and managed in an AOG unit structure. The AOC is made up of personnel from the AOG and personnel from the associated headquarters. The ANG augmentation is provided to staff the AOC at a level at which it is able to handle continuous operations beyond a short-term response or crisis. However, the present manning of active AOGs is about 40 to 60 percent, which means that the augmenting ANG unit is very much part of the basic AOC capability.

first option of a centralized reachback location. The natural systems and manpower redundancy in this option would help mitigate the single-point risk of terrorist attacks or natural disasters.

This option would also widen the recruitment footprint and allow some flexibility in assigning personnel with specific-area skills that may be more abundantly located in any one area—for example, personnel with intelligence experience are available in the Washington, D.C., area, but may not be as freely available in other parts of the country. It could also help to retain mission knowledge within a broader slice of the ANG constellation. Therefore, the mission may become less isolated and more a part of the broad mission focus of the ANG.

Centers of Excellence

The final option evaluated involves distributed process. Separate geographic locations would work separate missions, becoming experts in particular missions (see Figure 5.2). For example, a unit in Illinois could become the Center of Excellence in global mobility planning and analysis. Its location near AMC and U.S. Transportation Command Headquarters would assist in its developing deep knowledge in all aspects of mobility planning. Any combatant commander who had a mobility planning issue would subscribe to the services provided by that Center of Excellence. There could be many Centers of Excellence in many locations specializing in many missions; however, it would be more cost-effective to locate the Centers of Excellence where there are already established commercial or military infrastructure and experts, so that accessions would be less complicated and positions for ANG personnel might be available within the active mission or mission support structure (for example, schoolhouse and standboard functions). These centers could be developed as a result of a need expressed through the combatant command for AOR/mission issues, or from a specific ANG outreach to a more generic need (for example, WMD analysis and civil support).

Figure 5.2
Notional Configuration of Centers of Excellence

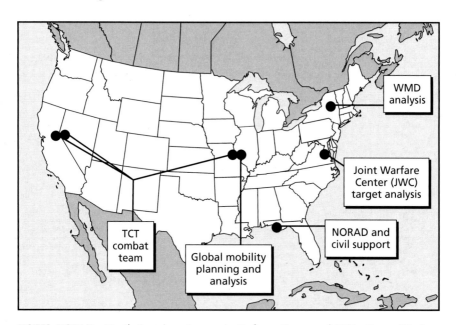

NOTES: NORAD = North American Aerospace Defense Command; TCT = time-critical targeting.
RAND *MG375-5.2*

Cost Analysis

In evaluating the costs, benefits, and risks of each of the three reach-back options, we took such factors as facility costs (per-square-foot cost of the infrastructure) and communications costs into consideration. Units supporting the AOC by augmentation already have some level of training infrastructure in place. Depending on the unit, a good bit of this already meets Sensitive Compartmented Information Facility (SCIF) quality standards, which is more expensive and needed for AOC reachback.[12] However, current augmentation units

---

[12] The cost of SCIF and other secure space is more expensive to create and takes a significant lead time to gain the necessary certification. The Falconer AOC requires a SCIF and other secure space. The functional AOC secure space varies with mission and task. Once tasks are identified, then the facility costs can be easily computed.

are not resourced for the full AOC Training Suite.[13] There would be a smaller cost to complete the infrastructure at existing sites than to develop a new site.

We also considered communications costs, such as bandwidth, for secure and unsecure voice and data lines, as well as the savings from moving tasks back to CONUS that would have required such forward operation location support as tents, services, security forces, and the airlift used to transport personnel forward. Temporary-duty assignment costs are also factored into the overall costs.[14]

Costs

We first evaluated facility costs. The Air Force Civil Engineer Support Agency's *Construction Cost Handbook* (2004, p. 9) states the cost of a new headquarters facility is $181 per square foot. Using an average of 15 square feet per person, the one-time facilities costs come to $2,715 per person for new construction of new facilities. The infrastructure costs would remain relatively constant whether one reachback site or multiple sites were used. If, however, existing facilities were used, there may be opportunities to reduce the investment cost. There would be upgrade and/or renovation costs, but not new infrastructure costs. There could be some additional savings in personnel if all COMAFFORs/JFACCs reached back to one site. The additional personnel savings would generate some facilities savings, although this amount was generally negligible.

Next, we considered communications costs. The difference between adding a communication line overseas and adding one in CONUS is significant. For example, a new lease for a T1 satellite link from Washington International Terminal to Prince Sultan Air Base, Saudi Arabia, has a monthly recurring cost of $45,800 and a non-recurring cost of $10,000. If reachback were used and a new T1 Integrated Services Data Network (ISDN) communication line was

---

[13] The AOC Training Suite comprises the software and computer support found in the Falconer AOC.

[14] Not included in the cost analysis is manpower. We did not evaluate cost for active, Reserve, and blended units.

installed at an established CONUS base, the monthly recurring cost would be only $2,021, plus a nonrecurring cost of $5,000.[15] The communications costs would remain fairly equal whether one reachback site was used or several: Either multiple lines would be added at one site or one line would be added at multiple sites.[16]

The next large cost considered was for systems used in the AOC. Each AOC Training Suite, already in place at several CONUS locations, costs approximately $2 million.[17] If reachback incorporated those sites that already have this system architecture, there would be only relatively minimal upgrade costs. If reachback were established at a location that does not already have the AOC Training Suite, a one-time cost of approximately $2 million would be required at each reachback location to establish a baseline capability. Again, if reachback were to only one location or to several locations, the cost would remain approximately the same. Each COMAFFOR/JFACC would need a Training Suite to reach back to—whether in several rooms at one location or in several different facilities. Note that the Training Suite is essentially the same equipment as the operational capability, albeit more limited in function. Discrete federal work (Title 10 tasks) could be accomplished today using the training equipment and software systems.

Savings

Reachback does offer several opportunities for Total Force cost savings. First, we consider deployment savings in terms of transportation costs. For our purposes, we assumed that the annual deployment cost is approximately $56 per person per hour of airlift. We obtained that number by taking the cost of a commercial 747 ($18,648 per hour)

---

[15] Data are from ACC/SCC.

[16] There may be some savings from locating reachback missions near existing high-bandwidth national users. One AOC augmentation unit is located within a microwave hop of a large National Geospatial-Intelligence facility. Use of other national assets would require special access and letters of agreement, but such assets could provide a lower-cost means for connecting the reachback unit to the distributed communications systems being used by the warfighter.

[17] Data are from ACC/DOYC.

and dividing it by the number of passengers it can carry (335). Depending on the number of people deployed, the number of deployments per year, and the number of flying hours to the forward location, the cost savings of reachback could be considerable.

The same is true for sustainment savings. Using an Air Force–accepted planning factor of $30 per day, the number of people forward times the days deployed times the number of deployments a year could add up to substantial savings using reachback. Neither the deployment nor the sustainment would be greatly affected by the number of reachback locations. Only the flying time for one location versus another location would affect the savings. Likewise, the longer ANG personnel stay in place, the lower the transportation cost. Deployment in-garrison on a reachback mission makes almost all these direct and indirect costs null.

AMD Example

In our analysis of the AMD, we determined that the tasks *receives validated requirements* and *assigns air mobility assets to meet the requirement* could be accomplished via reachback. In the AMD, the Airlift Control Team, the Aerial Refueling Control Team, and the Air Mobility Element perform these tasks. To calculate the number of personnel to move back to CONUS, we looked at the manning document from Al Udeid Air Base (2004) as an example. There are 35 personnel in the Airlift Control Team at Al Udeid Air Base. We left five personnel forward (the liaison officers [LNOs] and personnel associated with ATO production) and brought the remaining 30 personnel back to CONUS. There are eight Aerial Refueling Control Team members at Al Udeid Air Base. We left these personnel forward because of the dynamic nature of their work processes. There are three personnel in the Air Mobility Element; we brought all three personnel back to CONUS. In all, we determined that 33 positions could be moved back to CONUS to perform these two tasks.[18] Table

---

[18] In discussing this analysis with senior leaders, we learned that there may be some adjustments to the number of personnel eligible for reachback support once the Air Force evaluates the tasks and functions performed by these individuals. In addition, there may be

5.1 breaks out the costs and savings for one year of moving those 33 personnel back to CONUS.

In establishing the AMD functions in the rear, the one-time facility cost would be approximately $90,000. As mentioned previously, this cost could be less if existing infrastructure was used. The new T1 communication line would cost $5,000 initially and then $24,000 annually. Again, if existing communication lines are used, this cost could decrease.[19] Systems are by far the largest investment. If

Table 5.1
Sample Cost Savings Using Reachback for AMD Functions

Factor		One-Time Investment	Cost
Personnel	33 people		
Facility cost	$181 per foot 15 ft per person	$89,595.00	
New T1 comm requirement	MRC: $2,021 NRC: $5,000	$5,000.00	$24,252.00
Systems	$2M per Training Suite	$2,000,000.00	
Deployment transportation	$56 per hour per person 20 hr flying time (each way)		–$295,680.00
Sustainment	$30 per day per person 90-day rotation		–$356,400.00
	TOTAL	$2,094,595.00	–$627,828.00

NOTES: The deployment and sustainment figures assume four AEF rotations per year. MRC = monthly recurring cost; NRC = nonrecurring cost.

some economies of scale by moving positions back to CONUS. For example, there may be savings in the rear in the Air Mobility Element and in management positions. Forward, there could be economies of scale in communications and supply personnel. This analysis can easily adjust for any change in numbers of personnel provided by the Air Force.

[19] More use of tools such as Really Simple Syndication, text messaging, and a very assertive intra-AOC (forward and reachback) information management strategy could help control the bandwidth creep and costs associated with reachback capability. Just reducing the number of personnel forward will help control the amount needed.

an existing training site is used, the $2-million system cost would be greatly reduced.[20] Moreover, there is substantial savings for both deployment transportation and sustainment costs if reachback is employed. Approximately $296,000 for deployment and $356,000 for sustainment could be saved using reachback.

Over ten years, there could be a one-time investment cost of approximately $2 million counterbalanced by the $6.28-million savings in deployment transportation and sustainment. Adding in tent savings of approximately $675,000,[21] we conclude that the overall savings of using reachback in the AMD could be approximately $5 million over ten years.[22] In summary, there may be a large one-time investment, depending on where the reachback site is located, but overall, there are substantial savings per year using reachback to perform the tasks in the AMD.

DT/TST Example

In our analysis of the COD, we determined that at least a portion of the DT/TST team formed around the kill chain could be accomplished via reachback.[23] The DT/TST execution process works and collaborates with personnel in the other process-organized divisions. They also must closely coordinate activity with the on-site ISRD and Collection Manager to ensure access to sufficient sensors and other information necessary to prosecute the critical work process of find, fix, track, target, engage, and assess.

---

[20] Cost reduction is not additive, since each person would need a workstation and access to software for the task no matter where they sit.

[21] One BEAR 550f set costs $5.624 million, which provides tents for 550 persons. Using these figures and assuming a tent life span of five years, we obtained a tent cost of $10,225 per person multiplied by 2 for a 10-year approximation.

[22] These savings do not include yearly maintenance costs for infrastructure and communications.

[23] This analysis is based on the assumptions we made using the Reachback Decision Tree. In discussing this analysis with senior leaders, we learned that there may be some adjustments to the number of personnel eligible for reachback support once the Air Force evaluates the tasks and functions performed by these individuals. This analysis can easily adjust for any change in the number of personnel provided by the Air Force.

Looking at manning documents used during USAFE's exercise Austere Challenge 2004, we determined that 25 DT/TST COD full-time, direct DT/TST-coded personnel (working two shifts) could be moved back to CONUS to perform DT/TST work processes. By limiting the personnel to only COD DT/TST-coded personnel, the analysis is very conservative.[24] We also assumed that the technical support (communications and systems) will remain at the remote site. Likewise, we assumed that, wherever the reachback mission is located, it will have the baseline communications support to meet its needs.

It is also assumed that the DT/TST reachback capability will operate as part and under the authority of the forward AOC subscribing to their service. As such, no additional mission overhead is associated with the mission, although there will be the normal Title 32 command and administrative overhead for this mission. (We assumed that such overhead would be bundled with other AOC reachback services and that this structure could be limited.)

Given the need for a DT/TST presence on the Offensive Operations floor, we concluded that, of the 25 personnel, there would need to be one DTO per shift. (This is the peacetime configuration.) It would be prudent to back up the DTO with a targeting technician, a DT/TST radio operator/technician (2E652; Sgt), and a DT/TST systems administration support technician. Thus, a total of four persons per shift would be needed in the forward area. This staffing would provide a visible focal point on the Combat Operations floor within visual range of the Offensive Operations Team Chief with his team. Some of this staffing could be reduced, depending on the situation and the ability to leverage communications and systems support from the AOC infrastructure. If so, the minimum number would be at least two.

With sufficient systems capability and reachback communications, the remaining 21 DT/TST-tasked personnel (the original 25 minus 4 working forward as described above) would be located with the reachback unit, providing support. During Austere Challenge

---

[24] This number does not include any personnel leveraged from the ISRD or combat plans division. It also allows a presence to continue on the Combat Operations Employment floor.

2004, two of the 25 were DT/TST-dedicated Joint Surveillance and Target Attack Radar System (JointSTARS) workstation operators. It is assumed that the JointSTARS data would be available remotely. Otherwise, these personnel would have to be within the line of sight of the JointSTARS platform. Although not used in Austere Challenge 2004 and therefore not reflected in the above numbers, other ISR platforms with the ability to provide remote data would also be located with the reachback DT/TST capability. These positions would be better located with the bulk of the analysts working the DT/TST problem, to help with cross-cueing and handing off target information between platforms. The manpower figures should include two more platform workstation operators (for systems/future systems other than JointSTARS).

Therefore, the number of personnel associated with a reachback capability for DT/TST would be 23 (the original 25, minus 4 working forward as described above, plus 2 personnel to other platform workstations). Each would have access to sufficient bandwidth and systems workstation capability to accomplish their specific tasks. As mentioned, this figure covers only the COD DT/TST personnel. Additional savings could be obtained if planning, strategy, and a coupled DT/TST ISR capability were added to the reachback mission configuration.

ISRD-assigned personnel are also involved in the DT/TST process. Collocating the DT/TST reachback with direct access to senior intelligence duty officer (SIDO) team members would provide increased situational awareness and flexibility to meet surge requirements during certain phases of operations, such as close air support (CAS) or combat search-and-rescue (CSAR) activity. Given the greater flexibility of reachback, some SIDO team members could be dual-tasked to meet these requirements. Meeting surge commitments in a crisis becomes a scheduling problem, not an activate, deploy, and work issue, and it makes using ANG manpower trained in DT/TST tasks easier.

Currently, the reachback exploitation being done with Global Hawk sensor data indicates that having a single platform LNO; a planner, working with the AOC Collection Manager; ATO builders;

and employment officers is sufficient to ensure that mission planners have access to the tasking data and that the DT/TST execution team has access to dynamic—real-time—intelligence technician analysts. Placing an LNO with the reachback capability would raise the number in reachback by two and ensure that sufficient mission planning information was passed to the forward-based ATO planners. (If more AOC activity were located at the reachback location, it may not be necessary to have a platform LNO at both locations.)

This brings the numbers to four forward and 25 in reachback (the original 25, minus 4 working forward, plus 2 working other platform workstations, plus 2 LNOs). The baseline model was Austere Challenge 2004 adjusted as stated. Table 5.2 breaks out the one-year costs and savings of moving those 25 personnel back to CONUS.

Establishing the DT/TST functions in the rear incurs a one-time facility cost of approximately $68,000. As mentioned previously, this cost could be less if existing infrastructure was used, especially if the existing space was secure space. The new T1 communication line would cost $5,000 initially, then $24,000 annually. Again, if existing

Table 5.2
Sample Cost Savings Using Reachback for DT/TST Functions

Factor		One-Time Investment	Cost
Personnel	25 people		
Facility cost	$181 per foot 15 ft per person	$67,875.00	
New T1 comm requirement	MRC: $2,021 NRC: $5,000	$5,000.00	$24,252.00
Systems	$2M per Training Suite	$2,000,000.00	
Deployment transportation	$56 per hour per person 20 hr flying time (each way)		−$224,000.00
Sustainment	$30 per day per person 90-day rotation		−$270,000.00
	TOTAL	$2,072,875.00	−$469,748.00

NOTES: The deployment and sustainment figures assume four AEF rotations per year. MRC = monthly recurring cost; NRC = nonrecurring cost.

communication lines are used, this cost could decrease. Systems are by far the largest investment. If an existing data-exploitation site is used, the $2-million system cost would be greatly reduced. There are substantial savings for both deployment transportation and sustainment costs if reachback is employed: approximately $224,000 for deployment and $270,000 for sustainment.

Over ten years, the approximately $2-million one-time investment would still provide savings when balanced with the approximately $4.7-million savings in deployment and sustainment.[25] When tents savings are factored in,[26] the overall savings over ten years would be approximately $3.2 million. As with the AMD, there may be a large one-time investment, depending on where the reachback site is located; but, overall, there is substantial savings using reachback to perform the tasks in the DT/TST.

The baseline Falconer AOC DT/TST tasks are still evolving. Work is being done at Nellis AFB and Hurlburt AFB to capture the lessons learned from using DT/TST reachback support during OEF and OIF. The biggest change from how DTs/TSTs were prosecuted in the past is the role of unmanned aerial vehicles (UAVs) and U-2 sensor exploitation—working with forward DT/TST command elements from a reachback location.

This initial look at the reachback issue did not examine qualitative factors, such as a commander's wish to have more of a forward presence, affecting costs and manpower. However, in the DT/TST example, we did allow for a forward presence with the command element in the AOC to help provide a more agile response when necessary. Trying to achieve sufficiently high command trust and confidence in the reachback DT/TST team quality decision drove us to leave sufficient presence forward. There are other issues that need to be addressed before the ANG expands its reachback mission.

---

[25] These savings do not include yearly maintenance costs for infrastructure and communications.

[26] One BEAR 550f set costs $5.624 million, which provides tents for 550 persons. Using these figures and assuming a tent life span of 5 years, we obtained a tent cost of $10,225 per person multiplied by 2 for a 10-year approximation.

Other Reachback Issues

Whether the ANG is tasked with the augmentation mission or a reachback mission, other implications of reachback must be considered. The current arrangement for augmentation is different from other force-level presentation. People and their knowledge are often more important than technology or systems. In the 125-person UTC for AOC augmentation, there is only one person with a Space AFSC. It can be difficult to keep that one space expert current in his field if he has no one else in his unit in the same field. Having only one-deep positions can make career progression more difficult.

Another consideration that needs to be addressed relates to the nature of in-garrison work. In order to conduct reachback tasks from home, the mission would have to change from one of *training* to one of *doing*. There are Title 10 (federal work) and Title 32 (state work) consequences in changing the workload. As an example, 1AF has dealt with many of these issues in their North American Aerospace Defense Command (NORAD) mission. Currently, ANG personnel (Title 32 personnel) are working a federal (Title 10) mission. The manner in which they handle the Title 10/Title 32 issues may be a good model for other missions to follow.[27]

There are also gaining command–support command relationships that would have to be resolved. Who would be responsible for infrastructure, systems, and manpower investment? All things considered, it is most important not to put the ANG in a position in which the mission they accept could become obsolete. The goal should be to improve warfighter support while exploiting the ANG strengths.

---

[27] ANG personnel at 1AF work in a Title 32 training status until an operational threshold is met. Once that operational threshold is crossed, personnel convert to a Title 10 federal status.

ANG Mission Strategy

Operational-level command and control is clearly a core Air Force activity that requires mature and experienced personnel to accomplish effectively. It is also a rapidly changing area. The ANG should look at the mission area as a broad one and manage its participation as such. This means funding ANG positions in key force-building institutions, such as the Weapons School, doctrine, standboard, and readiness training unit (RTU) activity, to name a few examples. These would be full-time positions engaged in the work of the organization and not ANG advisors, except for the fact that they are ANG personnel. This engagement would allow the ANG to continue to build knowledge over the operational command and control missions area, as well as provide career-progression opportunities for top experts. As the missions change and evolve, these personnel would be positioned to best understand the effect on the ANG and help prepare the ANG for the next evolutionary step. Figures 5.3 and 5.4 illustrate two examples of where we feel the ANG could position itself with respect to reachback and enabling functions for the long-term: using reachback to support the AMD mission and to fulfill the DT/TST mission via reachback, respectively.

Both reachback missions rely on enabling functions, such as planning and policy, training, and support infrastructure. By involving ANG personnel in the enabling functions, as well as in the mission itself, some of the issues faced under the current augmentation arrangement would be resolved, such as the conflict between gaining and supporting commands. Having personnel involved in doctrine development or by serving on a Combat Air Force Headquarters staff could put ANG personnel in positions where they could keep current in their fields. It may also aid in career progression. An individual could start out in the DT/TST reachback cell, move to a training or instructor position, then come back to lead the DT/TST cell—all in CONUS.

Figure 5.3
Notional AMD Mission Support via Reachback

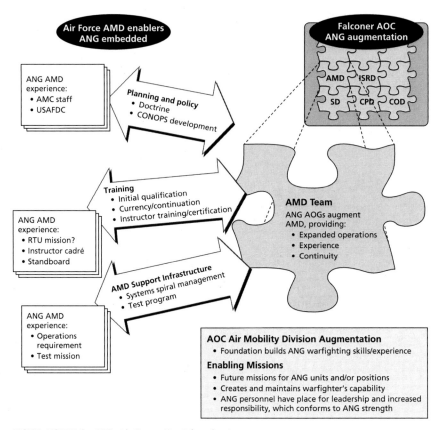

NOTE: USAFDC = U.S. Air Force Doctrine Center.

Figure 5.4
Notional DT/TST Mission Support via Reachback

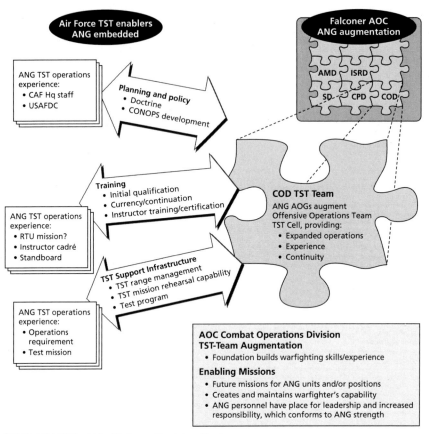

NOTE: USAFDC = U.S. Air Force Doctrine Center.
RAND MG375-5.4

Figure 5.5 shows a notional example of how the ANG could physically position itself in the AMD reachback mission. This is just one example of how a constellation could be set up around the AMD mission in CONUS. ANG personnel would be involved in the mission itself, as well as in the enabling functions related to the AMD mission. There are many ways this constellation could be established. The same is true for the DT/TST mission (see Figure 5.6).

Figure 5.5
Notional ANG AMD Reachback Constellation

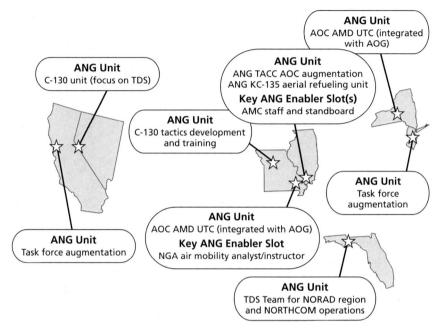

NOTES: TDS = theater distribution system; NGA = National Geospatial-Intelligence Agency; NORTHCOM = U.S. Northern Command.
RAND MG375-5.5

Figure 5.6
Notional ANG DT/TST Reachback Constellation

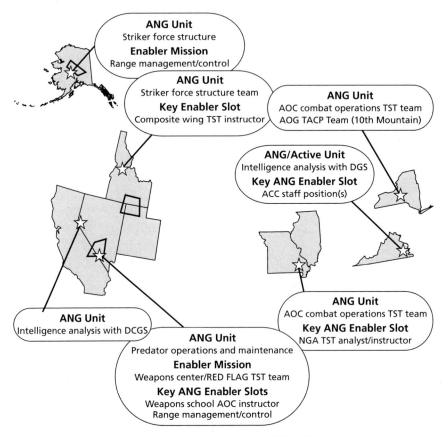

NOTES: DCGS = distributed common ground station; NGA = National Geospatial-Intelligence Agency; TACP = tactical air control party.

Air Force and ANG Reachback Implications

The AOC augmentation arrangement currently being used, whereby ANG augmentation personnel deploy forward, is valuable. The operational-level command and control mission is key to warfighter effectiveness and an important core Air Force capability. In this phase of the research, we have also seen where partnering has increased ANG acceptance, provided a strong advocate for systems and equipment, and created a strong mission partner within the warfighter community. We have seen that connecting an ANG unit to a theater adds value through unit ability to gain knowledge of operations and situational awareness. ANG units can be especially valuable because of the strengths of experience and civilian skills. Over time, the ANG could maintain the theater corporate knowledge.

The transformation concept discussed in this section takes augmentation one step further—establishing reachback to infrastructure and/or personnel for products and services to which the AOCs could subscribe. In moving specific tasks and services back to CONUS, ANG strengths are utilized and a place for deep knowledge and backup is developed. Reachback moves the ANG away from augmentation and into providing AOC capabilities on-site. This move may save on deployment and sustainment costs while requiring an initial investment in infrastructure to include communications and systems. Consolidation at one reachback location may offer some economies (for example, AOC-context information management expertise and information technology help). There are, however, implications for moving to reachback. The current unit organization assumes augmentation. This new concept would require new CONOPS and placing ANG in positions to gain knowledge, adding value to the warfighter.

One should not minimize the concern of senior leaders of not having direct face-to-face authority over personnel. One reason for selecting the DT/TST example was to better understand the trust, confidence, and oversight/insight balance that geographic location affects. The RAND Decision Support Tool (Reachback Decision Tree) will help approach candidate tasks in an objective manner and record the governing assumptions for later analysis. Our analysis found many key tasks, many of them very time-sensitive, being accomplished from a reachback location. More work needs to be done to better understand the doctrine, organization, training, materiel, leadership, and personnel (DOTMLP) consequences of reachback. Our DT/TST and AMD discussions with commanders, both ANG and active, did indicate that AOC supervisors need much more visibility into who is doing AOC work. A tool similar to what the intelligence community uses to manage requests for intelligence is necessary to help commanders in dealing with reachback confusion.

In this analysis, we have identified two new potential mission areas for the ANG. To assume these new missions, the ANG must establish work processes for ANG personnel to do federated work on a regular basis. Federal work can be done and is in fact being done today. However, Title 10/Title 32 issues need to be addressed and the ANG needs to come up with a range of tools and approaches to deploy in-garrison, to do Title 10 work, and to work under proper authority (federal or state).

Active duty personnel are interested in gaining full-time Guard technicians as currently used by NORAD and in 1AF. There are several examples of the use of Guard personnel in federal work. The ANG should establish a standardized process to use Guard personnel in a federated manner on tasks that are under the authority of Title 10 personnel, without UTC activation; then, as new missions arise, the Guard is ready to accept them. From our understanding, it is simply a matter of establishing a letter of authorization or establishing a policy by which personnel can change status to federal work. Once the ANG has a process in place, whether it requires changing the law or not, Guard personnel will be in a position to accept new missions involving federal work.

CHAPTER SIX

Summary and Conclusions

The goal of this analysis was to evaluate ANG capabilities to achieve the required effects specified in Air Force CONOPS that support DoD Strategic Planning Guidance (SPG). From there, we investigated transformational opportunities for the ANG that would add the most value in achieving the desired operational effects. In this research, we investigated four Air Force areas of interest: modified CE Establish the Base UTCs and a new Sustainment UTC, CONUS CIRFs, enhanced GUARDIAN combat support planning capability, and operational command and control reachback options.

In the civil engineer (CE) analysis, we found that modifying some CE UTCs, changing the deployment concept, and creating a separate Sustainment UTC might better support the AEF mission. The modified UTCs would provide intense CE support during a shorter deployment, to establish the base. Then a separate UTC would provide sustainment. These concepts could reduce active deployment requirements, as well as deployment and sustainment costs.

The CONUS CIRF analysis highlights several findings. First, small flying units with small intermediate-level maintenance (ILM) operations can be inefficient, making such operations a prime candidate for transition to a CIRF. Economies of scale would suggest that one, or at most a few, large CIRFs for each commodity might be the best option, potentially offering substantial cost savings without degrading weapon-system support. However, large CIRFs might be difficult for the ANG to staff from some local-area labor markets.

133

Second, transportation costs and transit times do not seem to significantly govern the CIRF location decisions. Therefore, for commodities for which adequate inventories are available, there is flexibility in the geographic location of the CIRF. However, for commodities that do not have an inventory to support transit pipelines, the ability to consolidate ILM may be limited.

Large bases will be strong "mini-CIRF" candidates, providing home-station support as well as ILM for a few small units. These large bases generate a large portion of the demand for ILM. The ANG could negotiate with the active duty Air Force to staff all or a portion of these mini-CIRF maintenance complexes. The workload, supporting peacetime steady-state operations and then quickly shifting to contingency operations, would be well suited for a blended ANG/AFRC/active duty staffing rather than relying on civilian contractors.

The Force Structure and Cost Estimating Tool (FSCET) could be a useful combat support planning extension of GUARDIAN. It provides an initial capability to examine ANG fleets' airworthiness, operational suitability, availability and O&S costs. Because the tool is script-driven and because fleets can be defined as needed by the using organization (for example, to the base level), the current FSCET data set and rules could be reconfigured to examine ANG-unique issues. At a minimum, the tool would also help the command estimate the consequences of the coming changes in force structure and operational tempo, thereby supporting the development of the command's inputs to the POM and the longer-range AFCIS.

During the reachback analyses, we found that the currently used AOC augmentation arrangement is valuable. It has postured state ANGs, units, and personnel to take the step toward deployed in-garrison work. Reachback does pose some challenges for commanders and AOCs as they are currently structured in the forward area, and it will require some additional costs and investment in personnel. However, in moving specific tasks and services back to CONUS, ANG strengths are utilized and a place for deep knowledge and backup is developed. This initial RAND research has provided a tool (Reachback Decision Tree) and an analytic framework for evaluating AOC tasks for reachback.

Reachback moves the ANG away from augmentation and into providing AOC capabilities on-site. This move may save on Total Force deployment and sustainment costs while requiring an initial investment in infrastructure, to include communications and systems. Consolidation at one reachback location may offer some economies (for example, AOC-context IM expertise and IT help), although not significant ones.

There are, however, implications for moving to reachback. This new concept would require new CONOPS and changes in the way the ANG operates traditional ANG units (Title 32 ANG personnel working Title 10 federal missions). We did note that the augmentation approach and regional partnership did create strategic partners in the overseas MAJCOMs (USAFE and PACAF) to help champion and work out these key issues.

In each of these areas, CE Establish the Base, CONUS CIRFs, FSCET, and AOC reachback, potential ANG participation has been evaluated and a marginal cost analysis has been provided. Each of these areas could offer other potential options of interest. The four areas evaluated were meant to be inclusive, not exclusive. The capability-based-analysis approach that was used in the four areas evaluated can be extended to identify other ANG capabilities.

Project AIR FORCE, at RAND, can work with the ANG to establish an analytic framework to guide internal transformation efforts. An approach similar to that taken during the Chief of Staff Logistics Review (CLR) could be used to identify opportunities for ANG transformation to better meet the AEF mission. And using such a framework, RAND could help the ANG find tasks that can be accomplished to leverage ANG strengths while mitigating limitations.

Any transformational opportunity will require an ANG champion to develop the concept and negotiate mission requirements with the active duty Air Force. As provided in this monograph, the ANG can choose from a range of options. Each is likely to require negotiation with the active duty Air Force to determine the extent of participation.

As evidenced in this monograph, there are several mission areas, such as CONUS CIRFs and AOC reachback, in which the ANG could add value to the warfighter.

Reachback Decision Tree

For the reachback analysis in this monograph (see Chaper Five), we developed a tool for nominating potential reachback candidates. This tool is a decision tree (see Figure A.1), which can be applied to any task or mission. The decision tree consists of a series of questions to which the user answers yes or no. The answer to a question routes the user down the tree until the end of a branch is reached. At that point, the task will either be offered as a potential candidate or eliminated for reachback. The decision tree itself is a Microsoft Access database that tracks a user's answers and provides a way to capture comments and/or assumptions about the questions and/or answers.

Figure A.1
Reachback Decision Tree

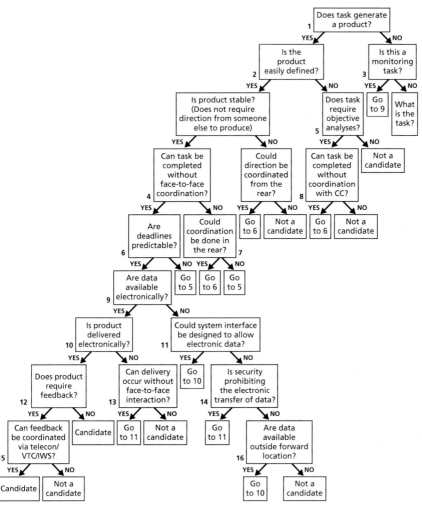

RAND *MG375-A.1*

Bibliography

AEF Libraries, maintained at the AEF Center, Langley AFB, Va.

Air Force Civil Engineer Support Agency, Directorate of Technical Support, *Historical Air Force Construction Cost Handbook,* Tyndall AFB, Fla., February 2004.

Al Udeid Air Base Air Mobility Division Manning Document, spreadsheet, from Deputy DIRMOBFOR and AMD Director, 15EMTF/CV, dated April 2004.

Amouzegar, Mahyar A., and Lionel A. Galway, *Supporting Expeditionary Aerospace Forces: Engine Maintenance Systems Evaluation (En Masse): A User's Guide,* Santa Monica, Calif.: RAND Corporation, MR-1614-AF, 2003.

Amouzegar, Mahyar A., Lionel A. Galway, and Amanda Geller, *Supporting Expeditionary Aerospace Forces: Alternatives for Jet Engine Intermediate Maintenance,* Santa Monica, Calif.: RAND Corporation, MR-1431-AF, 2002.

Amouzegar, Mahyar A., Robert S. Tripp, Ronald G. McGarvey, Edward W. Chan, and C. Robert Roll, Jr., *Supporting Air and Space Expeditionary Forces: Analysis of Combat Support Basing Options,* MG-261-AF, 2004.

Austere Challenge 2004 Joint Manning Document, spreadsheet, USAFE/AF, dated March 19, 2004.

Clark, Major Willard, "WFHQs Briefing—Directors Update," briefing, April 28, 2005.

Dahlman, Carl J., *Setting Requirements for Maintenance Manpower in the U.S. Air Force,* Santa Monica, Calif.: RAND Corporation, MR-1436-AF, 2002.

Feinberg, Amatzia, H. L. Shulman, L. W. Miller, and Robert S. Tripp, *Supporting Expeditionary Aerospace Forces: Expanded Analysis of LANTIRN Options,* Santa Monica, Calif.: RAND Corporation, MR-1225-AF, 2001.

Galway, Lionel A., Mahyar A. Amouzegar, R. J. Hillestad, and Don Snyder, *Reconfiguring Footprint to Speed Expeditionary Aerospace Forces Deployment,* Santa Monica, Calif.: RAND Corporation, MR-1625-AF, 2002.

Galway, Lionel A., Robert S. Tripp, Timothy L. Ramey, and John G. Drew, *Supporting Expeditionary Aerospace Forces: New Agile Combat Support Postures,* Santa Monica, Calif.: RAND Corporation, MR-1075-AF, 2000.

Geller, Amanda, David Geroge, Robert S. Tripp, Mahyar A. Amouzegar, and C. Robert Roll, Jr., *Analysis of Maintenance Forward Support Location Operations,* Santa Monica, Calif.: RAND Corporation, MG-151-AF, 2004.

Headquarters U.S. Air Force (HQ USAF/ILGD), CIRF CONOPS Transportation Computation Chart, spreadsheet, 2004.

Leftwich, James A., Robert S. Tripp, Amanda Geller, Patrick H. Mills, Tom LaTourrette, C. Robert Roll, Jr., Cauley Von Hoffman, and David Johansen *Supporting Expeditionary Aerospace Forces: An Operational Architecture for Combat Support Execution Planning and Control,* Santa Monica, Calif.: RAND Corporation, MR-1536-AF, 2002.

Loredo, Elvira, Raymond Pyles, and Don Snyder, "Programmed Depot Maintenance (PDM) Capacity Assessment Tool: Workloads, Capacity, and Availability," unpublished RAND research, 2005.

Lynch, Kristin F., John G. Drew, David George, Robert S. Tripp, Charles R. Roll, and James Leftwich, *The Air Force Chief of Staff Logistics Review: Improving Wing-Level Logistics,* Santa Monica, Calif.: RAND Corporation, MG-190-AF, 2004.

Lynch, Kristin F., John G. Drew, Robert S. Tripp, and C. Robert Roll, Jr., *Supporting Air and Space Expeditionary Forces: Lessons from Operation Iraqi Freedom,* Santa Monica, Calif.: RAND Corporation, MG-193-AF, 2005.

McIntosh, C. R., TF-34 briefing, OC-ALC/LR, 2004.

Peltz, Eric, H. L. Shulman, Robert S. Tripp, Timothy L. Ramey, Randy King, and John G. Drew, *Supporting Expeditionary Aerospace Forces: An Analysis of F-15 Avionics Options,* Santa Monica, Calif.: RAND Corporation, MR-1174-AF, 2000.

Pyles, Raymond A., *Aging Aircraft: USAF Workload and Material Consumption Life Cycle Patterns,* Santa Monica, Calif.: RAND Corporation, MR-1641-AF, 2003.

RAND Corporation, CIRF OOB, spreadsheet, 2004.

Sherbrooke, Craig C., *METRIC: A Multi-Echelon Technique for Recoverable Item Control,* Santa Monica, Calif.: RAND Corporation, RM-5078-PR, 1966.

Sleptchenko, A., M. C. van der Heijden, and A. van Harten, "Effects of Finite Repair Capacity in Multi-Echelon, Multi-Indenture Service Part Supply Systems," *International Journal of Production Economics,* Vol. 79, 2002, pp. 209–230.

Snyder, Don, and Patrick Mills, *Supporting Air and Space Expeditionary Forces: A Methodology for Determining Air Force Deployment Requirements,* Santa Monica, Calif.: RAND Corporation, MG-176-AF, 2004.

Sperry, Kenneth, *KC-135 Economic Service Life Study (ESLS),* Witchita, Kan.: The Boeing Company, Technical Report EA 00-023R2-135OTH, 2001.

Tripp, Robert S., Lionel A. Galway, Paul S. Killingsworth, Eric Peltz, Timothy L. Ramey, and John G. Drew, *Supporting Expeditionary Aerospace Forces: An Integrated Strategic Agile Concept Support Planning Framework,* Santa Monica, Calif.: RAND Corporation, MR-1056-AF, 1999.

Tripp, Robert S., Lionel A. Galway, Timothy L. Ramey, Mahyar A. Amouzegar, and Eric Peltz, *Supporting Expeditionary erospace Forces Concept for Evolving to the gile Combat Support/Mobility System of the Future,* Santa Monica, Calif.: RAND Corporation, MR-1179-AF, 2000.

Tripp, Robert S., Kristin F. Lynch, John G. Drew, and Edward W. Chan, *Supporting Air and Space Expeditionary Forces: Lessons from Operation Enduring Freedom,* Santa Monica, Calif.: RAND, MR-1819-AF, 2005.

U.S. Air Force, *Centralized Intermediate Repair Facility CIRF Test Report,* AF/ILMM, June 21, 2002a.

————, *Flight Manual, Air and Space Operations Center, AN/USQ-163-1, Falconer,* Vol. 1, Rev. 7, November 26, 2002b.

————, *Operational Procedures: Air and Space Operations Center,* Air Force Instruction 13-1, Vol. 3, June 1, 2002c.

————, *Command Posts,* Air Force Instruction 10-207, May 16, 2003.

U.S. Air Force, Force Modules, XOA, February 2004.

U.S. Air Force, Manpower and Equipment Force Packaging (MEFPAK), XOXW, February 2004.

U.S. Air Force, Air Combat Command, *A/OA-10 Engine Regional Repair Center ERRC and Jet Engine Intermediate Maintenance JEIM Analytical Report,* HQ ACC/XP-SAS, February 1998.

U.S. Air Force, Air Force Materiel Command, *Combat Logistics Support,* AFMC Instruction 10-202, September 24, 2001.

U.S. Air Force, Air Mobility Command, *AMC Command and Control Operations,* AMC Instruction 10-207, Vol. 1, February 13, 1995.

————, *CONOPS for Air Mobility Division Air National Guard Augmentation,* Scott AFB, Illinois, March 27, 2004.

————, *Director of Mobility Forces (DIRMOBFOR) Policy and Procedures,* AMC Instruction 10-202, Volume 7, August 1, 2004.

U.S. Air Force, Customer Service and Career Enhancement (DPMP), Consolidated Manpower Database (CMDB), September 2003.

U.S. Air Force, Oklahoma City Air Logistics Center, *Engine Handbook,* 2002.

U.S. Air Force, Pacific Air Forces, *Command and Control Operations Procedures,* PACAF Instruction 10-601, December 7, 2001a.

————, *Pacific Air Mobility Operations,* PACAF Instruction 10-2101, April 13, 2001b.

————, *PACAF Command Posts,* PACAF Instruction 10-207, October 10, 2003.

U.S. Air Force, U.S. Air Forces, Europe, *USAFE Command Posts,* United States Air Forces Europe Instruction 10-207, December 31, 2003.

U.S. Air National Guard, *VANGUARD Engagement Strategy,* December 2002.

U.S. Department of Defense, *Quadrennial Defense Review,* Washington, D.C., 2004a.

————, *Strategic Planning Guidance,* Washington, D.C., 2004b.

U.S. Department of Defense, Military Surface Deployment and Distribution Command, *DoD Standard Transit Time–Truckload,* Washington, D.C., 2004.

The White House, *FY2003 President's Budget,* Washington, D.C., February 13, 2002.